Dave Doroghy a

T0270173

111 Places
in Vancouver
That You Must
Not Miss

(111)

emons:

Good teachers can "Rock the World" and make a big difference. Like my grade 11 and 12 English teacher Fran Beckett, who taught me how to right, I mean write. My only "B" after five years of "D" ridden report cards came from her. She was encouraging, positive, creative, and funny. I only wish that she was still with us to mark this book of short essays. D. D.

To Dr. Evils' father. Not only did he invent the question mark, he had the sort of general malaise that only the genius possess and the insane lament. G. M.

© Emons Verlag GmbH
© Photographs by Dave Doroghy and Graeme Menzies, except:
1700 Dunbar (ch. 1): David Kincaid;
Beaucoup Bakery (ch. 7): Yinger Wong;
Gulf of Georgia Cannery (ch. 37): Jesse Hebert;
Living Roof (ch. 62): Vancouver Convention Center;
Long Table Distillery (ch. 63): Long Table Distillery;
Museum of Anthropology (ch. 68): Cory Dawson;
Rogers Arena (ch. 86): Vancouver Canucks Archives;
Shameful Tiki (ch. 91): Greg Tjepkema;
Stir Coffee House (ch. 100): Rob Lowe
© Cover icon: shutterstock.com/jennyt
Layout: Eva Kraskes, based on a design
by Lübbeke | Naumann | Thoben
Edited by Karen E. Seiger
Maps: altancicek.design, www.altancicek.de
Basic cartographical information from Openstreetmap,
© OpenStreetMap-Mitwirkende, ODbL
Printing and binding: Grafisches Centrum Cuno, Calbe
Printed in Germany 2023
ISBN 978-3-7408-2150-0
Revised third edition, December 2023

Guidebooks for Locals & Experienced Travelers
Join us in uncovering new places around the world at
www.111places.com

Foreword

Our first collaboration was just over a decade ago in the years building up to Vancouver's hosting the 2010 Winter Olympic Games. Although we had different roles, we were both on the same team and shared many challenges, laughs, and deadlines leading up to this worldwide event. The same can be said for this project – a team effort all the way!

But even among teammates there is always some friendly competition. In this case, the creative challenge was for one of us to find some way to surprise or amuse the other when reviewing a story. There was no greater compliment than to hear the other say, "I did not know that!" Or to make each other laugh out loud. So we encouraged and brought out the best in each other, as every good team should. As a lifelong resident of the city, Dave was able to use his personal experiences and many local friendships to highlight the things only a long-time resident would know – like where to find the last vestige of Vancouver's NBA franchise, how to find the mysterious stone carvings along the Stanley Park Seawall, why the Toys "R" Us sign is weird, or whether there was any truth to the rumour that one of America's biggest Country stars got her big break in Vancouver. A keen history buff and curious researcher, Graeme enjoyed many hours discovering local places connected to the likes of Harry Houdini, the botanist from Captain Vancouver's ship, royalty from Hollywood's Golden Era, rock stars, hippies, and tycoons.

Working sessions, split between Dave's houseboat and Graeme's condo, were complemented by several 'photo safaris' – driving around the city in Dave's classic Morgan or his Westfalia, depending on the weather – and provided enjoyable opportunities to compete together for the best angles on a story or a photograph.

The result, we hope, is a collection of 111 Places that will amuse and entertain you, either by tickling your funny bone or by revealing something new about Vancouver that you may not have known before.

– DD and GM

111 Places

1 1700 Block of Dunbar

Turn-of-the-century time capsule homes

Hardly any streets remain in Vancouver that can authentically transport you back in time. Walk down the 1700 block of Dunbar Street, though, and you are truly revisiting a bygone era. Stand anywhere on that block and, other than the parked modern cars, very little has changed in the last 108 years. Most streets in Vancouver have either a mixture of old and new houses, or as the trend to gentrify neighbourhoods continues, new condos. This unique block on Dunbar is nothing but pure, unaltered 1911.

That's the year that builder Samuel Wellington Hopper began constructing the 10 big, beautiful homes that still line both sides of the street today. Hopper was born in Ontario on March 8, 1872. According to the city's residential permit records, he purchased all 10 lots at the turn of the century, and the homes cost between $3,000 and $7,000 each to build. Every one of them is a glorified two-story version of the California bungalow, which was popular at the time. Of note are the elevated balconies and distinctive roof dormers.

Back in 1911, the original occupants on the street were an interesting mixture of active and retired building contractors, entrepreneurs, a clergyman, and a physician. The house at 1725 Dunbar, although not the prettiest on the block, has some historical significance. Canadian photographer J. P. Spalding, who was born just a few years after Hopper, lived there for over 30 years. He purchased it in 1927 and ran a postcard and photography business from his home. Colour photography hadn't been invented at the time, and his wife hand-tinted her husband's postcards. The images on them depicted urban scenes of major cities and some of the most magnificent landscapes in Western Canada.

Spalding died in 1958, and the house was split into a duplex 40 years ago. Oddly enough, a professional photographer that was born the year he died owns half the house today.

Address Dunbar Street between 1st and 2nd Avenues, Vancouver, BC V6R 3L9, www.maltwood.uvic.ca/spalding/introduction.html | **Getting there** By car, street parking available | **Hours** Unrestricted from the outside only | **Tip** Banyen Books & Sound opened in Vancouver in 1970 long after the Dunbar houses were built. It is Canada's most comprehensive metaphysical bookstore and just two blocks away from the old row of houses (3608 West 4th Avenue, Vancouver, BC V6R 1P1, www.banyen.com).

2 _ 55 Dunlevy Avenue
From metal foundry to foodie fantasy

Built in 1924 for the Reliance Foundry Company, this railway district building located near the shipping docks is now a hidden treasure that foodies (and wine-ies and beer-ies) love to discover. Home to Postmark Brewing, Vancouver Urban Winery, and Belgard Kitchen, the building's inhabitants offer a triple-threat feast for all the senses. Remnants and artefacts of the building's blue-collar origins add character and warmth to this hidden hideaway that is part factory, part medieval castle, and has occasionally comforted and entertained stars of the big screen (Woody Harrelson), the small screen (Camila Mendes), and stage (Lady Gaga).

The first thing you notice when approaching the building is the odd collection of wooden posts sticking up between the sidewalk and the building. What's up with that? Leftover wood scraps? Modern art? Actually it's a tribute to the early history of the neighbourhood, whose roads are so old they were once made out of wood. Look around the street outside and you may see a patch on the road where the asphalt has come away and the old wooden road is exposed. The next things you'll notice are the enormous entry doors designed by Vancouver designer Omer Arbel (he also designed the windows). And if that didn't get your attention, there's another set of ginormous doors just inside the building, believed to originate from a church in South America.

Once past those doors it's not uncommon for first-time visitors to be momentarily stunned by sensory overload: sounds and smells from a busy kitchen, the fireplace, the couch, the kegs … and that huge steel winch that reminds you this was once one of Vancouver's earliest metal foundries. Commonly referred to as the Settlement Building, this is a place where the tradition of transforming raw materials into things of substance and beauty is being kept alive but in an entirely new way.

Address 55 Dunlevy Avenue, Vancouver, BC V6A 3A3, +1 (604) 699-1989, www.belgardkitchen.com, info@settlementbuilding.com | Getting there By car, the closest Impark lot is located at 611 Alexander Street | Hours Mon–Fri 11:30–close, Sat & Sun 10am–close | Tip Gastronomists will also enjoy The Mackenzie Room nearby, which also serves some of the best cocktails in town. Doors open at 5pm nightly (415 Powell Street, Vancouver, BC V6A 1G7, www.themackenzieroom.com).

3 Alibi Room

From fur traders to movie stars

Vancouver beer lovers worth their hops know about the Alibi Room. But while they have understandably been focused on the 50 different local and imported brews, many remain blissfully oblivious of the century-old building's colourful past.

Back in the early days, this beer connoisseur's paradise was once a fur trader's warehouse. Subsequent occupants included a glove manufacturing company and a confectionery. But things really changed in the late 1960s when local entrepreneur George Pately thought the joint would be the perfect place to bring back the roaring twenties with a new venue, The Banjo Room. Maybe he was inspired by the 1967 Hollywood movie, *The St Valentine's Day Massacre*, or by news that the Chicago warehouse where the massacre occurred was being torn down. In any case, Pately arranged to buy seven barrels of bricks from the 'kill wall' and have them featured in his bar. Unfortunately, patrons found the wall to be a little bit creepy. So the bricks were relocated to the men's room, and Pately redirected his promotional zeal toward another bizarre feature of the place: Canada's largest circular barbecue.

Eventually The Banjo Room closed and gave way to a watering hole called the Archimedes Club, used by the Vancouver Taxi Owners Association. (What a Greek mathematician has to do with taxi drivers remains a mystery.) The Alibi Room emerged in the late 1990s when Vancouver-born actor Jason Priestley joined forces with actors Gillian Anderson and Tom Skerritt to create a place where creative independent film types could hang out. Ownership has since changed, but the movie scripts, typewriters, and film projectors that decorate the interior remain part of their vision. So if you feel the need for some inspiration, this just may be the place to visit. The bullet-riddled bricks are long gone, but the walls still seem to have stories to tell.

Address 157 Alexander Street, Vancouver, BC V6A 1B8, +1 (604) 623-3383, www.alibi.ca | Getting there By car, metered parking is available on Alexander Street | Hours Tue–Thu & Sun 4–11pm, Fri & Sat 4pm–midnight | Tip Two blocks east on Alexander Street, you'll find Ask For Luigi, one of the best and most charming Italian restaurants in all of Canada. Go for the daily pasta (305 Alexander Street, Vancouver, BC V6A 1C4, www.askforluigi.com).

4 Archibald Menzies' Bust
The bronzed botanist beckons

Chosen by George Vancouver to be chief scientific officer aboard HMS *Discovery* on its five-year mission to explore strange new worlds, to seek out new life and new civilisations, and to boldly go where no man has gone before, Archibald Menzies (1754–1842) was the botanist who played Spock to Captain Vancouver's Kirk. At least, he was until the ship's surgeon died and he became Bones. Then again, considering Menzies was Scottish, maybe Vancouver just called him Scotty. In any case, Menzies was critically important to achieving the *Discovery's* mission.

Menzies' bronze bust, resting silently here among the colours and scents of the formal rose garden at VanDusen Botanical Garden, is now waiting to be discovered by you, along with his amazing botanical legacy. During his four-month botany blitz in the Pacific Northwest, he packed the ship with more than 250 terrestrial plant species. You can see some of these when you walk around VanDusen's 55 lush acres. There are plenty of Douglas fir trees (*Pseudotsuga menziesii*) to admire, and many of his other discoveries like the red alder (*Alnus rubra*) tree that Menzies documented in Discovery Bay, the western hemlock (*Tsuga heterophylla*) he found in Desolation Sound, as well as the Nootka cypress (*Xanthocyparis nootkatensis*) specimens which he collected while visiting Nootka Island.

The bust of Menzies is one of only two in the world. This original was created by Jack Harman in 1972. In 2020, his son Stephen cast a second bust, which is now on display at Castle Menzies in Scotland. Nearby stand two more busts created by Harman: Carolus Linnaeus (1707–1778), the Swedish genius responsible for the scientific taxonomy methods used by Menzies, and Scottish botanist David Douglas (1799–1834) for whom the Douglas fir is named. Trek over to VanDusen and experience the nexus between art, science, history, and our natural environment.

Address 5151 Oak Street, Vancouver, BC V6M 4H1, +1 (604) 257-8335, www.vandusengarden.org | Getting there By car, use the on-site free parking off 37th Avenue | Hours See website for seasonal hours | Tip The Shaughnessy Restaurant at VanDusen Garden (5251 Oak Street, Vancouver, BC V6M 4H1, www.shaughnessyrestaurant.com) offers a great brunch and lunch menu and beautiful, airy decor. Make a day of it in the garden!

5 Artillery Search Lights
Hidden relics of World War II

Sometimes mistaken for gun placements or bunkers, these two concrete structures were originally designed to help illuminate the approaches to the Port of Vancouver along the Strait of Georgia in the event of enemy attack by naval vessels or submarines during World War II.

The two towers are located close to the shore, below what used to be the series of three gun placements of Point Grey Battery (now the Museum of Anthropology). Those guns had a range of just under 13 kilometres – enough power to hit Bowen Island – and could fire at a rate of six shells per minute. In 1939, the Point Grey Battery was the most heavily armed of the five coast artillery forts built to defend Vancouver. The searchlights were controlled remotely from an observation post and boasted a brightness of some 800 million candle power, which, if you are not all that familiar with candles, is enough to illuminate a target about three kilometres away.

The only time a ship was hit by the Point Grey Battery guns was in 1942, when a shell fired over the bow of a delinquent fishing boat ricocheted on the water and hit a freighter. Oops!

The Royal Canadian Artillery used the lights and guns until 1948, at which point the guns were removed. They began to transfer use of the buildings to the University of British Columbia, which converted them into student residences. Today, the search lights are functional only as a canvass for graffiti artists. The towers are out of the way but actually not all that hard to find, and getting to them makes for a pleasant hike.

The simplest way to get there is to follow Trail 4 to Tower Beach, located just to the west of the Museum of Anthropology. At the bottom of the 70-metre descent down a well-maintained path, turn right and walk along the rocky beach (wear sensible shoes). Be forewarned: the beach access is 'clothing optional'.

Address Tower Beach, Vancouver, BC V6T 1X8 | Getting there By car, park at the Museum of Anthropology or the UBC Rose Garden Parkade | Hours Unrestricted from the outside only | Tip Once an exclusive dining lair for nearby UBC faculty, the Sage Bistro (6331 Crescent Road, Vancouver, BC V6T 1Z2, www.sage.ubc.ca) offers terrific views of the ocean, modern West Coast cuisine, and brilliantly preserved 1960s' architecture.

6 Baden-Powell Trail

Hikers' haven, hiding in plain sight

Vancouverites have never had to worry too much about finding ways to get back in touch with nature, and hiking around the mountains on the North Shore has been a favourite pastime for generations. Some trails existed before written history, some were initially created for commercial reasons, and some by design. The Baden-Powell Trail falls among the latter category, having been established in 1971 at the initiative of the Boy Scouts and Girl Guides of British Columbia. The trail's name and the date of its creation are both significant: the trail is named after Lord Baden-Powell, who was responsible for creating the worldwide Scouting movement, and the date marked the 100th anniversary of British Columbia joining Canada.

The trail runs an impressive 42 kilometres across the south-facing slopes of the North Shore Mountains from Horseshoe Bay on Howe Sound to Deep Cove on Indian Arm. Along the way, it crosses many interesting features and sights, including the Cleveland Dam at the south end of Capilano Lake (seen in *Dawn of the Planet of the Apes* and the *Smallville* TV series), and the historic Lynn Valley Suspension Bridge. From one end to the other, the Baden-Powell Trail covers a total of 1200 metres in elevation, the highest point being Black Mountain and the lowest being at sea level. Most people enjoy the trail the way one might enjoy a fine wine – a bit at a time, and not all at one go. But for those who enjoy a punishing challenge, there is the annual Knee Knackering North Shore Trail Run, which covers 30 kilometres of the trail in a single day. The fastest time to date is 4:32:03.

A favourite short hike, for those wanting something less extreme, is the 3.8-kilometre hike up to quarry rock near Deep Cove at the eastern end of the trail. The exposed rock face rewards visitors with a panoramic view over Indian Arm, a 20-kilometre-long glacial fjord left over from the last ice age.

Address Accessible at many different places across the North Shore, www.trailsbc.ca/loop/lower-mainland/hike-baden-powell-trail-42-km | Getting there Access the trail from Deep Cove. Park at Panorama Park. | Hours Unrestricted | Tip Donut aficionados should not miss the opportunity to check out the hearty creations offered by Honey Doughnuts & Goodies. You earned a dozen after hiking the trail (4373 Gallant Drive, North Vancouver, BC V7G 1L1, www.honeydoughnuts.com).

7__Beaucoup Bakery
Food that inspires

Underneath the Granville Bridge on Fir Street, Beaucoup Bakery offers the kind of delicious and authentic French pastries you'd expect to find and enjoy only in a Parisian patisserie. *Pain au chocolat, pain au raisins,* buttery croissants, *chausson aux pommes* are a few of the treats guaranteed to get your morning off to a good start. Savour a coffee from the Italian espresso machine, dig the hip jazz playlist, and soak in the European ambiance that pervades this hidden delight. The only thing missing is a copy of *Le Monde, Paris Match,* and a classic Citröen parked by the curb.

Owned by Betty Hung and her brother Jacky, Beaucoup Bakery was originally created by Vancouver designer, writer, entrepreneur, voyageur, and overall lifestyle icon Jackie Kai Ellis in 2012. Armed with a dream and a diploma from the École Gastronomique Bellouet Conseil in Paris, Jackie created a café experience that attracts dozens of francophones, francophiles, and foodies every day. Like the farmer in W. P. Kinsella's *Field of Dreams,* Jackie risked everything to make her passion become reality. So if you think the bakery is only about food, you're only getting half the experience. For Jackie, food fills the soul as well as the body – the whole process from imagination to creation to consumption provides balance and perspective to life. And you can tell when you visit Beaucoup that this intangible ingredient is mixed into everything.

While Jackie has moved on to new adventures, such as writing a best-selling memoir, *The Measure of My Powers,* the new owners are firm followers and have been at Beaucoup since the beginning. As the former head pastry chef, Betty maintains the bakery's high standards, and, more than that, the bakery is now helping her and Jacky to follow and achieve their own dreams.

Visit Beaucoup, and you'll be well fed and you will also be inspired.

Address 2150 Fir Street, Vancouver, BC V6J 3B5, +1 (604) 732-4222, www.beaucoupbakery.com, hello@beaucoupbakery.com | Getting there By car, free parking in the alley next to the bakery and metered parking on Fir Street | Hours Mon–Fri 9am–4pm, Sat & Sun 9am–5pm | Tip If you feel the need to walk or pedal off some calories, the most northerly point of the 8.5-kilometre Arbutus Greenway project begins just across the street (www.vancouver.ca/streets-transportation/arbutus-greenway.aspx).

8 Big Yellow Sulphur Pile
What on earth is that stuff?

Many residents of Vancouver have asked themselves for the last 50 years, "Just what is that huge pile of yellow stuff? And what is it doing here?" The pile can easily be seen from 30,000 feet in the sky when you fly over YVR and is best viewed from miles away on the south shore of Burrard Inlet or downtown. That pile, by the way, is around 80 feet high and weighs about 160,000 tons. It's sulphur of course.

Sulphur is a byproduct of the oil sands, and Alberta has an abundance of it. It is brought to BC by freight train and stored in that outdoor, open pile. There is a worldwide market for sulphur, which is used to make hundreds of products, like batteries, wine, shampoo, pesticides, and treatments for skin disease, to name a few.

The yellow element may be a bit of an eyesore, but don't ever call it a worthless pile. Today, a ton of sulphur is worth about $125. Fifteen years ago, it was worth only $20 a ton, until it had a huge spike when demand went up in 2009. Much of the sulphur on the North Shore is bound for Asia. China alone consumes about a quarter of the world's supply of sulphur every year, and the Vancouver harbour is well positioned to ship it there. Sulphur is always in demand somewhere, and the bright yellow mineral just sits there, waiting for huge ocean-bound freighters to carry it overseas. And then an endless line of freight train cars come in from the prairies to drop off a new load.

Just don't get too close to it while smoking. Sulphur is combustible and used to make matches, black gunpowder, and fireworks. You probably don't want to get too close to it anyway, since it has a slight odour of rotten eggs. Contrary to the popular myth, the sulphur from that pile is not used for dye in Crayola crayons. Vancouver is not, in fact, one of 12 cities that supplies a specific colour to Crayola. And San Francisco does not have a giant blue pile in its harbour.

Address 1995 West 1st Street, North Vancouver, BC V79 1A8, www.portvancouver.com |
Getting there Best view is from the north side of the Stanley Park Seawall | Hours
Unrestricted | Tip Another great way to see the pile – and more interesting than land
viewing – is from the seat of a sea bus. On the Vancouver side take the sea bus from the
Waterfront Station across the inlet to the Lonsdale Quay on the North Shore (123 Carrie
Cates Court, North Vancouver, BC V7M 3K7, www.translink.ca).

9_ The Billy

Badges, beers, and bombers

Entering the Billy Bishop/Kerrisdale Legion is a bit like stepping into a secret time machine. Walk down the rather ordinary looking street where it is located, find its very ordinary looking building, check your Google map to make sure you're really in the right place, and then make your way inside. Suddenly, you're in a cozy British pub that looks like it was frequented by airmen in the Battle of Britain. The transformation is miraculous. Some think Legions are only for veterans, but don't be mistaken: guests of legal drinking age are welcome to enjoy a cool pint at The Billy.

In fact, if the stories are to be believed, it seems three or four ghosts visit the place from time to time as well. Inside the pub, named after famous Canadian World War I Flying Ace William 'Billy' Avery Bishop, you'll find numerous tributes to the Victoria Cross-winning airman and his comrades. There are hanging models of the 1917 Nieuport 17C and the S.E. 5a he flew in 1918. Next to his portrait over the fireplace are badge plaques of the six units in which he served.

The Billy was established in 1945 by a group of Royal Canadian Air Force (RCAF) veterans, so it's no surprise there are plenty of authentic World War II artefacts all around. There are over 100 images on the walls – several framed prints by official war artists and some autographed by the air crew. The collection of over 500 regimental and squadron badges is the largest private collection in Canada. Over the bar rests a propeller from an Avro Anson twin-engine trainer. Another propeller sits over the piano. The fireplace grate is made out of connecting rods from a World War II aircraft engine. There's an amusing picture of Legion President Walter Buswood paddling through the lounge in a raft during the flood of 1967, a reminder that The Billy is the only place in the area that still sits at its original pre-settlement site elevation.

Address 1407 Laburnum Street, Vancouver, BC V6J 3W4, +1 (604) 568-4130, www.billybishoplegion.org, info@billybishoplegion.ca | Getting there By car, closest parking is at Kitsilano Beach (on Arbutus Street) or at nearby H. R. MacMillan Space Centre | Hours Wed & Thu 4–8pm, Fri & Sat 4–11pm, Sun 3:30–8pm | Tip Beautiful Kitsilano Beach, home to some of the best sunsets and people-watching scenes in the city, is just a short 10-minute walk away (Cornwall Avenue at the north end of Yew Street, Vancouver, BC V6J V6K).

10 Blue Whale Skeleton

The biggest one in Canada is at the Beaty Museum

If you like big, rare, and aquatic things, you must visit the big blue whale bones at the Beaty Museum. The massive skeleton on display is the largest in Canada and one of only 21 complete such skeletons in the world on public display. These impressive bones, some 26 metres long and 80,000 kilograms in weight, are all that remains of a whale that washed ashore on Prince Edward Island in 1987, buried under the sand for 20 years, exhumed, 'degreased', and shipped to UBC, where it has been on display since 2010.

After you take in that awe-inspiring spectacle, browse through some of the over 500 natural history exhibits organised in the museum's six permanent collections. There are, in total, over two million specimens in the collection, and some items were first gathered over 100 years ago. The Cowan Tetrapod (Greek for 'four legs' – these are vertebrate animals that have, or whose ancestors had, four legs) Collection, for example, has over 40,000 specimens representing 2,500 species. Do you know what a red panda looks like? Have you seen the endangered Vancouver Island marmot, the inspiration for MukMuk, the first-ever official Olympic mascot sidekick? How about the now-extinct carrier pigeon? Duck-billed platypus? The largest collection of plants native to BC, Canada's third largest fish collection, and hundreds of thousands of insects are all here to dazzle and amaze you with the wonders of the natural world.

A popular feature of the Beaty is the 30-metre-long, horizontal Timeline Exhibit, which covers 4.54 billion years of the earth's history. Each step you take along the timeline represents 100 million years in time. And speaking of time travel, the movie *Tomorrowland*, starring George Clooney, was filmed nearby. So if you're picking up a New York 1964 World's Fair vibe during your visit, that's probably why.

Address 2212 Main Mall, Vancouver, BC V6T 1Z4, +1 (604) 827-4955, www.beatymuseum.ubc.ca, info@beatymuseum.ubc.ca | Getting there By car, closest paid parking is the UBC Health Sciences Parkade | Hours Tue – Sun 10am – 5pm | Tip Plenty more big bones can be seen across the mall at the Pacific Museum of Earth (6339 Stores Road, Vancouver, BC V6T 1Z4, www.pme.ubc.ca) where you'll find a 13-metre-long cast replica of an 80-million-year-old marine Elasmosaurus and more fossils, rocks, minerals, and gems.

11 __ The BowMac Sign
Large Signs "R" Us

In 1958, North America's largest freestanding sign towered above the sidewalk at 1154 West Broadway proudly advertising the BowMac car dealership below. The colossal 80-foot structure could be seen from 18 miles away and was one of the largest illuminated structures in the city.

Today, one might think that its 1,200 incandescent light bulbs and extensive colourful neon tubing would have seemed more at home on the Las Vegas Strip than in sleepy little Vancouver. But during the late 1950s, Vancouver was considered the neon capital of North America, with dozens of smaller artistic signs scattered throughout its early commercial urban landscape.

In the 1980s and 1990s, signage bylaws became stricter in Vancouver, and the outdated beacon began to stick out like a sore thumb. Some local residents considered it an earthquake hazard, others complained that it was noisy and contributed to unnecessary light pollution. Many local residents considered it nothing more than an old eyesore.

Controversy ensued, and the red, blue, and white sign almost ended up being demolished in 1997. That's when the City of Vancouver, under a Heritage Revitalization Agreement, stepped in and gave the giant toy store chain, Toys "R" Us, zoning approval to drape their logo over it. The BowMac sign was granted official protected status, so it is not going anywhere any time soon.

BowMac was short for Bowel-McDonald and later Bowell-McLean, and they sold Cadillacs, Pontiacs, and Buicks. Toys "R" Us is short for Toys Are Us, and they sell Barbie dolls, Lego, and video games in the shadow of the old giant sign. As traditional bricks-and-mortar retail gets replaced with more luxury condos in Vancouver, the long-term future of the sign is anyone's guess.

It's best to go see the sign in the light of day though. Although all the components are still intact, the sign has not been lit for years.

Address 1154 West Broadway Street, Vancouver, BC V6H 1G5 | Getting there By car, street parking available | Hours Unrestricted | Tip One of Vancouver's most iconic neon signs advertised the 1930s' Aristocratic Restaurant. A working copy of the sign, complete with the restaurant's cartoon mascot Ritsy, and their slogan 'Courteous Service, Quality Food, All Over Town', can be seen at its original location today. The corner however is now occupied by Chapters Indigo Books, which prominently displays the artefact in their front window (2505 Granville Street, Vancouver, BC V6H 3G7, www.facebook.com/indigogranville).

12 Brassneck Brewery

A witty West Coast whistle whetter

Vancouver has many excellent brewpubs and craft beer makers, but the tasting room at Brassneck is a hidden gem that you must experience. The rough-hewn wooden walls, the iron chairs, the brass pumps, cement floor, and steel pipes all set the stage for a whistle-whetting performance that stands apart from mainstream commercial brewers. Best of all, a visit to Brassneck is a visit back to a time when craft brewers just wanted to make great beer, not take over the world. Because, despite the popularity of the brand and the success of the product, the Brassneck owners have decided not to expand. This is it. This is their only location. It doesn't feel as much like you're in a bar, but rather like you're in your friend's basement. The conversations are casual, strangers become neighbours, the vibe is chill, and the stresses of the work day and the issues of the world melt away. Or maybe that's just the abbey-style Cherubesque Belgian beer kicking in.

And speaking of the beer, well there's that too. At any given time, whenever you visit, a handful of the favourites will be on tap together with a handful of surprises. So it's never the same place twice. The insanely creative brewers have developed nearly 100 brews since the establishment opened in 2013, each with a taste as remarkable as its name. Sometimes it's tempting just to order according to your mood. Maybe a Passive Aggressive or an Identity Crisis? Sometimes the names riff on their ingredients – the Magician's Assistant is a dry hopped tart blonde. If there's just too much choice, you can fill up a growler to enjoy at home.

For those who like to nibble on something tasty while they soak in the experience, six kinds of sausages and one kind (the big kind) of pretzel can be purchased indoors. If that won't do, there's often a food truck parked outdoors, and you can bring something to eat back to your table.

Address 2148 Main Street, Vancouver, BC V5T 3C5, +1 (604) 259-7686, www.brassneck.ca, info@brassneck.ca | Getting there By car, parking is available at Lot 17 (199 East 7th Avenue) | Hours Sun & Mon 2–10pm, Tue–Thu 2–11pm, Fri & Sat noon–11pm | Tip Just around the corner, The Whip is a great place to grab a bite and take in more of the Mount Pleasant neighbourhood vibe, and every Sunday at 4pm they uncask more Vancouver craft beers (6th Avenue, Suite 209, Vancouver, BC V5T 1J7, www.thewhiprestaurant.com).

13 Cartems on Main
Where history and donuts collide

There are few things more Canadian than donuts. So enjoying one in a building associated with British Columbia's transition from British colony to Canadian province is a treat too tasty to be denied to patriotic historians.

While Cartems Donuts' first official storefront was located on Pender Street, it is this one on Main that occupies a special place in Vancouver's – and Canada's – history. The brick building dates back to 1912 and was once owned by Israel Wood Powell, the doctor, businessman, and politician who was instrumental in leading BC toward union with Canada. Among his many roles and achievements, he is remembered for bringing the first Canadian flag to BC, which he presented to the Victoria Fire Department on July 1, 1871. He got the flag from his pal Sir John A. Macdonald, Canada's first prime minister.

Inside the building, Cartems occupies a space that was once visited by shoppers at the grocery store that was here a century ago and served the local community's needs. Below your feet, five layers of carpet and linoleum were removed to expose the original fir floors. The ancient wooden beams and reeded glass above the front windows draw your eyes up to the 12-foot ceilings. The setting is a fitting metaphor for their product: classic, simple, honest, cosy, and unpretentious donuts made with flour that comes from an organic mill in Chilliwack, milk from dairies in Abbotsford and Burnaby, and spices which are ethically sourced through a family-owned company on Cortes Island.

With all the exposed charm of this location, it's no surprise that the building has made cameos in several TV productions. The donut shop appeared – as a coffee shop – in the Bravo Channel production, *Imposters*, while one of the suites in the Ashnola apartments above the shop was Daniel's apartment in *Stargate SG1*.

Address 2190 Main Street, Vancouver, BC V5T 3C5, +1 (778) 707-1114, www.cartems.com, hey@cartems.com | Getting there By car, metered parking is available on Main Street and on East 6th Avenue | Hours Mon–Fri 7am–10pm, Sat 9am–10pm, Sun 9am–8pm | Tip If historical architecture dunks your donut, visit the Gene Coffee Bar, a short walk further south on Main Street (2404 Main Street, Vancouver, BC V5T 3E2, genecoffeebar.com). It's located in the iconic and triangular Wosk Block, a rare example of Streamline Moderne architecture.

14_Catfe
The cat's meow

Are you looking for that 'purr-fect' cup of coffee? Or maybe you just need a relaxing break from your hectic day, and nothing short of a full-on, fluffy, feline-friendly encounter will do. Cats just seem to bring out the best in us, but in today's busy world, having a cat of your own can be expensive and a bit of a hassle – after all, they need to be fed every day.

The Catfe on the border of Chinatown and Gastown in Vancouver has the solution. It's a hip coffee shop where you can sit among 8 to 12 laid back cats and enjoy some quality kitty time in a clean, odour-free lounge. Imagine the solace and comfort you'll achieve while you stir your coffee with one hand and gently pet a cat on the floor with your other hand, or sit with one on your lap as you sip a latte, or just observe them as they do what cats do, which is often nothing. Speaking of which, it's a good idea to go online and make a reservation, because sometimes the place shuts down for an hour to let the residents take a 'cat nap' to ensure they are fresh for the onslaught of adulation. Keep in mind that cats are more active in the morning, and it's not unusual to find them all snoozing in the afternoon sunlight. While you're online, you can also see who's who in the cat house, complete with each cat's name and a cute picture. You can't make this stuff up.

If you are not used to being around cats, don't worry. The friendly staff at the Catfe can instruct you on some subtleties to make them like you. First of all, you are not supposed to pick them up. That's right – you have to wait for them to jump onto your lap or somehow make the first move. And don't worry – there is even a handy brochure with tips on where they like to be touched.

All of the cats are from the BC SPCA and available to be adopted. If you just want a souvenir though, there is a gift shop with a small selection of 'meowchandise'.

Address International Village Mall, 88 West Pender Street, Unit 2305, Vancouver, BC V6B 6N9, +1 (604) 379-0060, www.catfe.ca, info@caffe.ca | Getting there SkyTrain to Stadium-Chinatown (Expo Line); by car, metered parking is available nearby | Hours Check website and book ahead | Tip Big cats – stone lions, in fact – guard the entrance to historic Chinatown, just a couple minutes' walk away (West Pender Street and Taylor Street, Vancouver, BC V6B 2T2). The female lion has her paw on a cub, and the male lion has a paw on a ball. Legend has it they both used to have polished granite balls in their mouths, but no one knows what happened to them.

15___Centennial Rocket Ship
Time passages

What's an old-fashioned, Flash Gordon-style, 12-foot-long space-ship doing in downtown Vancouver, and just how could it have land-ed there?

The Centennial Rocket, as it is known, has a long, storied past that is inextricably linked to the history of Vancouver. When the city was celebrating its 50th birthday, the Pacific National Exhibition staged a big Jubilee Parade. The year was 1936, and to help commemorate the special occasion, the Sheet Metal Workers Union Local 280 built a modernistic-looking rocket sculpture that was rested on a float in the parade.

After the parade, the rocket ship sat at the old airport termi-nal in Richmond, welcoming travellers from around the world until 1977. By that time, with all the rain we get in Vancouver, it had sadly rusted out and, like Flash Gordon himself, was fading into a distant memory. It's a good thing that the original designer of the sculpture, Lew Parry, had kept the original plans and diagrams of the rocket. In 1985, the same Sheet Metal Workers Union, along with the Van-couver Transportation Club, contacted him with the idea of building a new rocket to commemorate the city's 100th birthday. Only this time, the intergalactic symbol would be built to last. After its rebirth, it was temporarily displayed near its current location on the grounds of the Expo 86 World's Fair.

Has the rocket ever flown? Well, sort of. After the fair came to an end, the rocket was donated to the City of Vancouver and moved by helicopter to its current location near the Cambie Street SkyTrain Station. You can visit it there anytime you like, but you might want to wait until 2036. A special time capsule was put into the rocket that won't be opened till then, the city's 150th anniversary. It contains multiple artefacts from the era, including ten Expo 86 passes and recorded messages from various Vancouver celebrities.

Address 520 West 6th Avenue, Vancouver, BC V52 4H5 | Getting there SkyTrain to Olympic Village (Canada Line); by car, metered parking is available on Cambie Street | Hours Unrestricted | Tip If you are interested in the old space-age cartoon hero Flash Gordon or his contemporary Buck Rogers, there are two comic book shops not far from the Centennial Rocket on Main Street: Lucky's Books and Comics (3972 Main Street, Vancouver, BC V5V 3P2, www.luckyscomics.storenvy.com) and 8th Dimension Comics (2418 Main Street, Vancouver, BC V6A 3Y5, www.8thdimensioncomics.com).

16__City Farmer
Composting, cultivating, and computing

Good organic ideas, when nurtured with passion, knowledge, and patience, generally just grow and grow. When the City of Vancouver started allowing its residents to create small garden plots to plant food along an abandoned railway line, it was the good seed of an idea. So good, that over the years, the city added more and more vacant city properties, and before you knew it hundreds of small, individual, 6-by-12-foot plots were flourishing with home-grown vegetables.

Along with all those local residents tilling, fertilising, and watering the soil, obviously lots of good questions arose about gardening techniques and about just what to plant. Those questions sprouted into City Farmer, which is an amazing resource centre behind the railway tracks and manned with plant-smart, happy volunteers and paid staff teaching the locals how to grow food in the city, compost their waste, and take care of the environment. Classes, demonstrations, interpretive displays, workshops, books, and school field trips – it's all there in one welcoming building on three-quarters of an acre of plush vegetation in the middle of the city. Leave yourself at least an hour to see the climate adaptation garden, green roof, cob shed, organic food garden, permeable lane, natural lawn, water-wise garden, worm and backyard composters, beehive, and more. The transfer of knowledge is diverse, infectious and, of course, ever growing.

Ahead of its time, City Farmer grew into a web. Not as in the spider that crawls all over your string beans, but as in the Internet. City Farmers' executive director is a forward-thinking, computer-savvy man named Michael Levenston who developed the first website to ever publish information about urban farming. Two important websites thrive today, both originated from the newspaper publication *City Farmer* that began in 1978.

Address 2150 Maple Street, Vancouver, BC V6J 3T3, +1 (604) 736-2250, www.cityfarmer.info, www.cityfarmer.org, cityfarmer@gmail.com | Getting there By car, street parking available | Hours See website for seasonal hours | Tip Only in a city like Vancouver would you find Rolls-Royce Motor Cars of Vancouver a block away from the hundreds of earthy urban farming plots. Imagine a Phantom VII hauling a trunk full of compost (1809 West 5th Avenue, Vancouver, BC V6J 1P5, www.rolls-roycemotorcars-vancouver.com).

17_ Commodore Lanes

Canada's oldest bowling alley

Its glory days are mostly long gone. But if you haven't been to the Commodore, you're not only missing out on a really fun way to experience Vancouver's past, you're also missing out on some unusual sports history. The Commodore has many claims to fame: the oldest bowling alley in Canada; the first to rent bowling shoes; and the first to field a women's bowling league. The billiard parlour claims to be the last original pool hall of its kind in the city. If Jeff Bridges' character, The Dude, were from Vancouver, you know he'd abide in this place.

In fact, many celebrities and movie stars have abided in the Commodore since it opened its subterranean doors below the Commodore Ballroom in 1930. Legend has it that Hollywood cowboy Roy Rogers rode over on horseback from the Pantages Theatre for a few games in 1932. Some reports say he parked his horse Trigger outside. Some say he rode the horse down the stairs. In any case, he made a big entrance. Clark Gable (Rhett Butler in *Gone With The Wind*), Jack Benny (*The Jack Benny Show*), Buster Crabbe (*Flash Gordon*) are also known to have dropped by. The place remains popular today, and their old slogan still promises customers 'a place where pleasant days may be spent'.

Another quirky feature of this place is the fact that there is no modern ten-pin bowling; instead, patrons use the uniquely Canadian five-pin bowling style. Sports folklore credits Torontonian Thomas F. Ryan for inventing the five-pin game in 1909 after some of his customers complained that the ten-pin bowling balls were too heavy. So if big balls have always discouraged you from bowling, this might be the place for you. And, if you would like to play with more small balls, the Commodore also has many billiard tables, foosball tables, and pinball machines.

The Commodore is licensed, so you can drink a White Russian while you channel your inner Dude.

Address 838 Granville Street, Vancouver, BC V6Z 1K3, +1 (604) 681-153, www.commodorelanes.com, commodorelanes@yahoo.com | Getting there SkyTrain to Vancouver City Centre (Canada Line); by car, Pacific Centre Parking at 818 Howe Street | Hours Sun–Thu & Sat 11am–close, Fri 10am–close | Tip Bowl in vintage apparel from the eclectic collections at F as in Frank (2425 Main Street, Vancouver, BC V5T 3E1, www.fasinfrankvintage.com), or Mintage (1714 Commercial Drive, Vancouver, BC V5N 4A3, www.mintagevintage.com).

18 _ Coupe de Villa

A half-buried Cadillac right in his front yard

What would possess someone to cut a 1960 Coupe de Ville Cadillac in half and bury it in their front yard in an upscale Vancouver neighbourhood? Who cares! The tail fin installation along with the rest of the rusty metal artefacts you'll find at Steve Edmundson's house is weird, eclectic, definitely out of place, and well worth visiting. Sadly, Edmundson passed away in 2021, but his legacy remains.

In 1993, when he dissected and planted the classic piece of Detroit iron, he had no idea how the neighbours or city would react. Steve is a great storyteller and explains how the zoning bylaw inspector came by to measure it one day to ensure it complied with municipal residential housing bylaws. Someone must have tipped him off to the inspection, because to be prepared for the anticipated resistance he put a rake and shovel in the car's trunk and told them it was nothing more than an elaborate garden tool shed. Then there is the story about his inquisitive quest to understand how people really felt about his fabulous fins. To gauge public opinion, he set up a hidden baby sleeping monitor microphone on the car so he could eavesdrop on conversations as strangers strolled past it. His straw poll indicated that 80 percent were in favour and 20 percent against. But the best story took place years ago in the middle of the night when some poor guy totally high on acid stumbled by it with its tail lights blinking bright red and had what you'd call a freak out – an unfortunate incident where the luxurious Cadillac provided a 'bad trip'.

To keep the display alive and interesting, Steve painted the Caddy a different colour every couple of years. The latest iteration is white with a cool black motif painted on the trunk done by a local First Nations' graffiti artist. He also said that from time to time people would come by and drop off artsy pieces of heavy metal, some of which are on display at the ever-changing yard gallery.

Address 3056 West 6th Avenue, Vancouver, BC V6K 1X3, www.facebook.com/coupedevilla |
Getting there By car, limited street parking is available in the neighbourhood | Hours
Unrestricted | Tip Get more chrome in your diet at nearby Sunshine Diner (2649 West
Broadway, Vancouver, BC V6K 2G2) where life-size mannequins of Elvis, James Dean, and
Marilyn Monroe greet guests at this classic 1950s'-style Kitsilano diner.

19 CRAB Park

An urban park like no other

There are urban parks like Central Park in New York, or Hyde Park in London, and then there are urban parks like CRAB Park. Although it's much smaller, what makes this park even more urban than these bigger, more famous places is that it is full of urban action. From here, you can see cargo ships, cruise ships, pleasure boats, float planes, helicopters, and even trains coming and going across the water and around the shore. And yet, despite all of that constant activity, it is still a peaceful and tranquil place. Its name might make you think this is a place where a lot of crab meals were prepared, and maybe it was, but that's not why the park is called CRAB Park. Actually its original name was Portside Park. CRAB is an acronym for the Eastside citizen committee that lobbied successfully in the 1980s to 'Create a Real Available Beach' in the heart of what used to be the industrial centre of Vancouver. But everyone got so used to the 'crab' moniker that, in 2004, the city formally changed the name to CRAB Park at Portside.

Located on the north side of the tracks from Gastown, and mostly hidden from sight by the old buildings of yesteryear, CRAB Park has a history that goes back to the earliest days of Vancouver. From the Squamish, Musqueam, and Tsleil-Waututh peoples who navigated these waters in ancient times, to the mariners who sail cargo to and from ports around the world today, these eight acres of unspoiled waterfront have been at the centre of it all. Back in 1866, this was even one of the first unofficial ferry stations for the freelance ferry service operated by John 'Navvy Jack' Thomas. In addition to the unique city views afforded by its location east of downtown, the park has some artistic and historical memorials worth noting. Chief among them are the Downtown Eastside Missing Women Memorial Stone, a mosaic about the Komagata Maru and the Urban Indian Y2K Rock.

Address 101 East Waterfront Road, Vancouver, BC V6A 4K3, +1 (604) 257-8158, covapp.vancouver.ca | Getting there By car, closest paid parking is Impark lot no. 1216 on Main Street and East Waterfront Road | Hours Unrestricted | Tip Navvy Jack's home is still standing at 1768 Argyle Avenue in West Vancouver, just a short walk away from The Ferry Building Gallery (1414 Argyle Avenue, West Vancouver, BC V7T 1C2, www.ferrybuildinggallery.com).

20__Dark Table Restaurant
An out-of-sight place to eat

Have you ever wondered what dining would be like if you couldn't see the food that you were eating? Does taking away your sight enhance the other three senses of hearing, smell, and, most importantly in this particular situation, taste? You can find out for yourself when you dine at one of the most unique, interesting, and darkest restaurants in Vancouver.

The Dark Table Restaurant is built around a simple and well-executed concept. As the name suggests, the restaurant serves dinner in total darkness. It's not about mood lighting dimmed way down low. No – the restaurant has the same degree of pitch-blackness that you would find in an old-fashioned photographer's dark room. The quality of food served, though, is not compromised in any way.

When you arrive, before you are thrust into complete sightlessness, you get to select your dinner choices from a first-class menu. Once you are ready, a blind or visually impaired server will escort you to your table. After you are seated, it takes a while to adjust. Within a few moments, you start to smell things more acutely, and you begin to hear things more intensely. Then, when dinner arrives…. Well, you'll just have to experience it for yourself.

The restaurant's concept can be traced back to Switzerland and a blind man named Jorge Spielmann. He'd blindfold his dinner guests to demonstrate to them what eating was like for a visually impaired person. He claimed that his guests enjoyed the experience in that it amplified appreciation for the flavours. Aside from learning more about your senses at the Dark Table, you will also be supporting Vancouver's blind community. The tables are turned here, with the visually impaired servers leading those who are sighted throughout the entire experience. Just don't bring any modern devices with you that emit light. Even the luminous dial on your watch can ruin this remarkable experience.

Address 2611 West 4th Avenue, Vancouver, BC V6K 1P8, +1 (604) 739-3275, www.darktable.ca | Getting there By car, street parking available on 4th Avenue | Hours Daily, see website for seating times | Tip Visit the gift shop at the Canadian National Institute for the Blind Vancouver Office. The shop sells magnifiers, clocks and watches, reading aids, special lighting, and a wide variety of other items for anyone who is visually impaired (200 5055 Joyce Street, Vancouver, BC V5R 6B2, www.cnib.ca).

21 Deadman's Island

The most haunted island in North America?

You can't really visit Deadman's Island. The best you can do is walk up to the front gates and look past the searching eyes of the sentry guarding the entrance to the Navy base that has occupied the land since 1943. But just because you can't walk the land doesn't mean you shouldn't know what you're missing. And when you do know what you're missing, maybe you'd rather not walk the land after all ... because Deadman's Island is reputed to be one of the most haunted islands in North America.

Though it looks peaceful and serene today, this place was once the sight of a major bloodbath. Sometime in the 1700s – the exact date is unknown – some 200 Coast Salish warriors were massacred on the island following a raid by one of their local rivals. In subsequent years, it served as a burial site for the Coast Salish peoples. Except the deceased weren't buried – they were placed in cedar boxes resting on platforms in the trees. European settlers discovered the boxes, and by 1870 they had all been removed and buried in Stanley Park.

Ever the traditionalists, the new settlers of the 20th century retained the island as a cemetery for the city of Vancouver. British merchant sailors, Canadian Pacific Railway workers, victims of the fire of 1886 and the smallpox plague a decade later all rest on the island. Burials there stopped during World War II after the federal government gave the land to the Canadian Navy. The Navy Reserve base is called HMCS Discovery, after the name of George Vancouver's ship, which laid anchor near this site on June 13, 1792. Close your eyes and try to imagine what that would have looked like, and listen for a ghostly whisper from the past. While nearly impenetrable to the general public, Arnold Schwarzenegger was able to film bits of *The 6th Day* here, and a few episodes of *Danger Bay* and *MacGyver* were filmed on the base too.

Address 1200 Stanley Park Drive, Vancouver, BC V6G 3E2 | Getting there By car, parking is available 20 metres past the military base, at left. By bicycle, a Mobi Bike station is located at the parking area. | Hours Open for scheduled tours only, reservation required | Tip If naval history rings your bell, plan to visit the Vancouver Naval Museum located within the base (www.sites.google.com/site/vancouvernavalmuseum/welcome-aboard). Access is limited and only by appointment, but it's worth the effort – and it's free.

22 Dude Chilling Park

A great sign for a selfie

'Dude' is a modern name for someone who is cool. It is a masculine noun. 'Chilling' is another modern term that has taken on the meaning of just hanging out or relaxing. A few years ago, the Vancouver Parks Board, which is neither run by dudes nor very chill for that matter, decided to change the name of one of the city's Official Parks to Dude Chilling Park.

The park that has quietly existed in the Mount Pleasant district, three blocks east of Main, for decades always had the nondescript name of Guelph Park. In 1991 a wooden sculpture called *The Reclining Figure* was installed in the park. Many of the residents that lived in the area interpreted the sculpture as being 'a dude just chilling'. As the years went by, the concept of a dude chilling gained more and more steam. Then, in 2012, an artist named Victor Briestensky came along, and, maybe as a joke or a way to assert playfully the local popularity of the name, he erected a sign identical to the official green Guelph Park sign, only it read, *Dude Chilling Park*. The Parks Board took umbrage and removed the sign.

Here is where the story gets interesting and turns into an exercise in civic democracy. Shortly after the Parks Board removed the bogus sign, the people who live in the neighbourhood decided to do something about it and organised a petition with 1,500 names on it demanding that the name of the park be officially changed to Dude Chilling Park. It took a couple of years, but in 2014, the Parks Board voted to change the name of the park from Guelph Park to Dude Chilling Park.

Today, a local beer is called Dude Chilling Pale Ale, and the story of the park and how its name was changed has travelled far beyond Vancouver. American late-night talk show host Jimmy Kimmel remarked on the success of the Dude Chilling Park petition on his show, saying it may be a reason to move to Canada.

Dude Chilling Park

Address 2390 Brunswick Street, Vancouver, BC V5T 3L8, www.vancouver.ca/parks-recreation-culture/new-public-art-in-guelph-park.aspx | **Getting there** By car, street parking is available around the park | **Hours** Unrestricted | **Tip** Take home a bottle of Dude Chilling Park Beer as a souvenir of your visit, but first, drink a cold one at R and B Brewing Company (54 East 4th Avenue, Vancouver, BC V5T 1E8, www.randbbrewing.com).

23 Earnest Production Store

An urban oasis for ice cream aficionados

Earnest Ice Cream's popularity is spreading across Vancouver like a scoop of vanilla on a slice of hot apple pie, so it's much easier to find it now than when the company started just six years ago. But for the true ice cream aficionado, Earnest's production kitchen on Frances Street is the place to experience the epicentre of product development. Here you can reward yourself with a refreshing treat and get the satisfaction of tasting the very latest flavours and products. Try the new ice cream sandwiches, or sample some unique flavours, like Ghost Chocolate (made with cacao bean husks) or Spruce Bud (made from spruce trees).

If owners Ben Ernst and Erica Bernardi are around – and the odds are good that you'll find them there – you can even give them your personal review. Because they not only insist on using locally sourced ingredients from BC farms in their ice cream, they also insist on listening to customers as they develop their product. You can taste Earnest ice cream at any of their four scoop shops, but the production kitchen is special and worth the trip.

Ben and Erica created the production kitchen on Frances Street because the building had the large space they needed, and because they love the neighbourhood. They're not alone: craft breweries and distilleries dot the area along with boutique cafés, restaurants, and artist studios. There's also some interesting history to the location. Old maps of Vancouver show this as Keefer Street, but it was renamed in 1929 in honour of Vancouver's first public health nurse, Fanny 'Sister Frances' Dalrymple Redmond. In the middle of the road, you can see where the steel rails of the Georgia East Streetcar line once ran. A lot has changed since those tracks disappeared, but it's good to know there's still room in the city for good old-fashioned ice cream sold in glass jars by people who love what they do.

SCOOPS

please notify us of any allergies

Matcha Green Tea

Salted Caramel

London Fog

Cookies & Cream

East Van Roasters Ghost Chocolate

Spruce ...d

Mint Chip

Birthday Cake

Address 1485 Frances Street, Vancouver, BC V5L 1Z2, +1 (604) 428-2933, www.earnesticecream.com | Getting there By car, street parking on Frances Street is available | Hours Daily noon–10pm | Tip While in the neighbourhood, explore one of Vancouver's most diverse and innovative arts and cultural hubs, The Cultch (1895 Venables Street, Vancouver, BC V5L 2H6, www.thecultch.com).

24 The East Van Sign

A symbol of marginality and defiance

The East Side of Vancouver has always been a bit rougher and harder edged than the West Side. Things have changed in the last two decades. as neighbourhoods to the east of Main Street have become more gentrified with hip coffee shops, artist studios, and expensive, trendy lofts popping up. But back in the '60s and '70s, there was more of a socio-economic divide. Houses sold for less on the East Side, there were more railroad tracks and strip bars, and many of its neighbourhoods were working class. A rivalry existed between the two ends of town. And graffiti artists would tag the sides of buildings and buses with the slogan, "East Van Rules."

Some locals claim that the origin of that clever design, a vertical "East" with a horizontal "Van" resembling a cross, dates back to the '40s. Many people link the cross to the community's Catholic roots, as the East Side was home to many Eastern European, Greek, Italian, and Croatian Canadians of the Catholic faith. A gang called the East Enders, who were associated with the Hell's Angels, even adopted it as their club logo in the '90s. Today, the symbol appears on t-shirts, jewellery, hats, mugs, Christmas ornaments, and even scented candles. So, to say that the East Van Cross has a colourful and controversial past would be an understatement.

In preparation for the Vancouver 2010 Olympic Winter Games, local artist Ken Lum was commissioned to create a massive, 17.3-metre (57-foot) sculpture of the symbol. Lighting up each night, *Monument to East Vancouver* proudly stands at the intersection of Clark Drive and East Sixth Avenue.

Lum has since left the city and is now the chair of the fine arts program at the University of Pennsylvania. After the cross went up, columnist Douglas Todd wrote in the *Vancouver Sun*, "It's rad, it's bad, it's a bit mad," and then he called it a "tribute to a rich, rough and fading local past."

Address 2113-2173 Clark Drive, Vancouver, BC V5T 1E6, www.kenlumart.com/ monument-to-east-vancouver | Getting there By car, parking is available at VCC – Broadway Campus – Impark lot #865 (1155 East Broadway) | Hours Unrestricted | Tip The 49th Parallel Brewing Company sells a craft lager in 12-packs with the East Van Symbol on the label (1950 Triumph Street, Vancouver, BC V5K 1T8, www.parallel49brewing.com).

25 Engine 374

Once derailed, now delightful

She looks great today, but there was a time when this Canadian Pacific Rail (CPR) beauty was a neglected wreck. It began with her construction in Montreal in 1886. The brand new steam engine, fuelled by wood and with capacity to hold 2,800 gallons of water, immediately made its way to Port Moody, along the way becoming the first scheduled train to cross Canada. The next year, she became the first transcontinental train into Vancouver.

Garnished in laurels, festooned in all manner of celebratory materials, proudly sporting a portrait of Queen Victoria on her smokestack, and the words 'Ocean to Ocean' painted on her boiler, her arrival was a seminal moment in the city, for the country, and for the British Empire. She was greeted with cheers from citizens, with music from bands, and with whistles from ships in the harbour. But after that, it was all downhill. She laboured away, hauling passengers hither and yon for the next 30 years, until she was almost scrapped in 1915. Luckily, she was selected for a complete rebuild instead and managed to get another 30 years' service on the rails. But by 1945 she was exhausted, and the CPR decided to put her out to pasture. Feeling nostalgic, they retrofit her to resemble her original old self and donated her to the City of Vancouver. But the City, perhaps not knowing what else to do with her, hauled her out to Kitsilano Beach and left her exposed to the elements for 40 years.

Salvation came from local railway history enthusiasts, who seized upon the fact that Vancouver was hosting the 1986 World Exposition on Transportation and Communication. The result is what you see before you today – a beautiful engine, restored by the passion and determination of citizens and housed in the stately comfort of the historic Roundhouse building, and a piece of Canadian railroad history saved from ruin.

Address 181 Roundhouse Mews, Vancouver, BC V6Z 2W3, +1 (604) 713-1800, www.roundhouse.ca, info@roundhouse.ca | Getting there By car, metered parking is available on Pacific Boulevard and Davie Street; ferry to Yaletown Ferry Dock | Hours Daily summer 10am–4pm, winter 11am–3pm | Tip A number of businesses took root near the Roundhouse, and just a short walk away you'll find the Gray Block (1202 Homer Street, Vancouver, BC V6B 2Y5), a well-preserved 1912 commercial warehouse that was once used as a starting off point for 'exporting' booze into the US during the Prohibition era.

26__Fabulous Float Homes

Positive flotation

Altogether, there are about 700 floating homes in the Greater Vancouver area. Just what would possess anyone to pack up their belongings and furniture and cram them onto a wave-rocked, damp barge? It's hard to explain, but the laid-back marine lifestyle, a bent toward anti-conformism, and amazing views are a good place to start. The best way to get an introductory understanding of what float home living is all about is to visit a small marina on Granville Island, where 12 of these colourful and buoyant denizens of the sea form a vibrant and unique community. Sea Village can be found near Pier 32 and has been part of False Creek since the 1960s.

It is a bit of a fish bowl existence for the float homeowners living there with lots of tourists and gawkers asking questions. As a primer before you go, there are a few things to know.

BC has a long float home history. The first ones were shanty log cabins haphazardly placed on tree trunks and peripatetically moved up and down the coast, servicing saw mills and forestry operations. Today, moorage is at a premium and hard to find. Municipal zoning bylaws, stringent environmental regulations, safety restrictions, and the all-important issue of what to do with your sewage have all done away with the days when you'd simply tie up to a dock and call it home.

Some of the smaller, two-level float homes can be pretty tippy, and placement of large potted plants, pianos, and, for that matter, dinner guests can be a bit of a balancing act. Most of the float homes on Granville Island are positive flotation, meaning that they sit on large, stable, styrofoam floats encased in concrete. They can't sink but very rarely tip over. Tides that rise up to 15 feet a day are another concern for anyone who lives on the water.

And, FYI, the sewage from a float home is pumped into the same sewer that everyone else in Vancouver uses.

Address 1301 Johnston Street, Vancouver, BC V6H 3R9 | Getting there Bus 050 to 2nd Avenue near Johnston Street | Hours Viewable from shore only | Tip The Public Market on Granville Island was the first of its kind in Western Canada, and it paved the way for all the other markets when it opened in 1979. It is a must-see less than 500 yards from the float homes (1669 Johnston Street, Vancouver, BC V6H 3R9).

27 False Creek Ferries
Water you waiting for?

A lot of people think taking a ferry is just something you have to do in order to get from point A to point B over water. But taking the False Creek Ferry isn't a chore at all – it's something people actually want to do because it's fun. Today, over a million people ride these ferries each year.

Hop aboard one of the 17 mini-tugboats that bob and weave their way around False Creek, like children's toys in a bathtub, and you'll be taking a scenic voyage through one of the most interesting neighbourhoods in the city. From as far west as the Maritime Museum ferry dock to the Village ferry dock near Science World, and seven destinations in between, a round trip ride will give you some of the best views of some of the most scenic waterfront destinations in Canada's prettiest city. You'll pass beneath three of the city's bridges – Burrard, Granville, and Cambie – and see every kind of watercraft, from stand-up paddleboards to luxury yachts – if you love a boat ride, these ferries will not disappoint.

But it wasn't always fun. In the 1950s this area was the industrial heartland of the city, with sawmills, lumber operations, and a smattering of small port operations sprinkled throughout. That chapter came to an end in 1960, when a massive fire completely destroyed the BC Forest Products plant and much of the lumber industry in the area – about the size of four city blocks – literally went up in smoke. The creek's future was sketchy. There was even talk of filling it in with dirt. Yet despite the uncertainty of the situation, George McInnis went ahead and started False Creek Ferry here in 1982 anyway. It was a good call. Expo 86 was just about to happen, and it kickstarted the transformation of the north side of the creek. Twenty years later, the Vancouver 2010 Olympics transformed the former industrial south side area into millions of square feet of new real estate for the Athletes' Village.

Address 1804 Boatlift Lane, Vancouver, BC V6H 3Y2, +1 (604) 684-7781, www.granvilleislandferries.bc.ca, info@granvilleislandferries.bc.ca | Getting there Board at any ferry dock; check website for locations | Hours See website for schedule | Tip Get off at the Yaletown Ferry Dock, and you'll immediately find a tall, bronze sculpture with cut metal plates that cast a shadow of historical events onto the sidewalk. The positioning of the panels has been calculated so that the optimum contrast and focus on the pavement corresponds with the month, date, and time that each event occurred.

28 First Canadian McDonald's

McHistory is made outside the USA

Ray Kroc, the American founder of McDonald's, loved to use the expression, "When you're green, you're growing." And never did the burger chain experience more growth than in the halcyon days of the mid-1960s. That was when McDonald's had over 700 restaurants in the United States and was expanding at a rapid pace. As a first step toward global fast-food domination, Kroc decided to plant the first pair of Golden Arches in a foreign country. He chose Canada, and more specifically the city of Richmond, BC. Richmond was a new suburb of Vancouver to where McDonald's target market of young, busy families was moving in droves. Kroc also chose Richmond for the town's proximity to the airport.

On June 1, 1967, McHistory was made when McDonald's expanded into Canada. Back then, Number 3 Road in Richmond, where their first Canadian restaurant still stands today, was a thoroughfare sparsely populated by a Simpsons Sears department store and the occasional commercial store. A plaque by the front door commemorates the opening of the restaurant and the important role it played in the chain's amazing growth. Inside, a large video screen plays a looped film on the chain's history. Today, there are 1,486 McDonald's restaurants across Canada.

Much of McDonald's success in Richmond and around the world has been built on the youthful enthusiasm of its employees. Inside the Richmond McDonald's hangs another historic plaque that frames a chronological display of 12 McDonald's business cards. They all belong to the current restaurant owner and franchisee, Joe Guzzo, who began working for McDonald's as a crew kid in 1975 at the age of 15. As you read the title under each card, you can see a young man's ambition as he progresses up the corporate ladder. Today, Joe owns 12 McDonald's.

Address 7120 Number 3 Road, Richmond, BC V6Y 2C6, +1 (604) 718-1045 | Getting there
By car, closest paid parking is the Impark lot at 8120 Cook Road | Hours Open 24 hours |
Tip Right around the corner is the modern Richmond City Hall. A noteworthy feature is
a 12-foot, silver metal sculpture of a Fraser River sturgeon fish under a waterfall. You won't
find one of these protected species in your Filet-O-Fish sandwich (6911 Number 3 Road,
Richmond, BC V6Y 2C1).

29___Floating Gas Station
Fill 'er up at sea

In 1959, had you stood on the Stanley Park Seawall gazing out onto Coal Harbour, you would have spotted five colourful, floating gas stations gently bobbing up and down in a perfect row, each one of them fully operational, pumping out marine fuel to a steady stream of recreational and commercial vessels. In 1984 there were four. Today only one remains. Just as car gas stations are becoming more rare in the city, floating gas stations have almost entirely disappeared.

The area where the barges floated became known as Gasoline Alley. For the record, a Standard Oil barge first dropped its anchor there in 1935. The lineage of the company can be traced back to the current Chevron Barge that floats there today. The other four major oil companies that operated barges next to the original Standard Oil barge were Shell, Esso, Home Gas, and Texaco. Their bright logos adorning large, backlit signs that were attached to their roofs became well known landmarks in the busy Vancouver Harbour. It was quite a peculiar site, and one seen nowhere else in North America. Normally, fuelling stations are located closer to the shore, and the bulk gasoline is pumped in through pipes from the land. The floating gas stations of yesteryear and the one that remains today were, and are, totally self-contained.

The last remaining barge has a real name that very few people in Vancouver know. It's formally called the *Chevron Legacy*. The barge was actually built by Alaska Ship and Drydock Incorporated out of Ketchikan and towed to its current mooring spot in January of 2010, just in time for the Olympic Games. The gas station is capable of dispensing an overwhelming 50 million litres of marine fuel every year.

The durable Chevron Legacy has an estimated lifespan of over 50 years, ensuring that future Vancouverites will get a chance to observe what is left of Gasoline Alley for years to come.

Address Coal Harbour, best seen from the Stanley Park Seawall or Waterfront Road | Getting there Accessible by private boat | Hours Unrestricted | Tip There is only one traditional car gas station left in downtown Vancouver. The Esso at Burrard and Davie sits on a corner lot assessed at $36 million. Better fill your tank up there soon before it is torn down and turned into a condo (1205 Burrard Street, Vancouver, BC V6Z 1Z5).

30 __ Flying Angel Club
Sailors' solace

Tucked away on the north side of the railway tracks that separate Railtown from the waterfront, at what used to be the northern end of Dunlevy Avenue, lies one of Vancouver's oldest and most overlooked historic sites. Known today as home to The Flying Angel Club, this is the original office building of the Hastings Mill that was established nearby in 1865. The office was built later in 1906 but has remarkably avoided the usual forces of destruction, such as fire, neglect, and commercialization.

There have been some changes over the years – the original vault was converted into a fallout shelter during the Cold War era, for example – but much of the building is unchanged and original. The building's antique, 14-metre-long (47 feet) basement support beams are as strong today as the day they were first laid down. The original brass fireplace accessories still occupy the lounge area that was formerly the Port Manager's office.

Outside the building, letters on the front porch commemorate the four past owners: BCMTT (BC Mills Timber & Trading), HSM (Hastings Saw Mill), VHC (Vancouver Harbour Commissioners), and NHB (National Harbours Board), while a neon sign identifies the Flying Angels Seamen's Club. A few feet away stands a granite monument created by sculptor Gerhard Class in 1966. The sculpture is based on three abstract tree trunk forms and includes relief carvings that recall the site's logging and milling history.

The Seamen's Club traces its history back to the days of the tall ships and is the BC headquarters of a worldwide society providing for the spiritual, physical, and emotional care of seafarers and their families. Since the Port of Vancouver hosts some 2,400 ships every year, the club members keep quite busy. Their mission reaches out to and hosts about 14,000 seafarers from 80 countries around the world annually.

Address 401 East Waterfront Road, Vancouver, BC V6A 4G9, +1 (604) 253-4421, www.flyingangel.ca, m2svancouver@gmail.com | Getting there By car, drive down East Waterfront Road to no. 401. Closest paid parking is the Imperial Parking Location no. 1216 at Main Street and East Waterfront Road. | Hours See website for information on visiting | Tip Just south of the railway tracks, you can get a great cup of coffee and healthy comfort food at Railtown Cafe (397 Railway Street, Vancouver, BC V6A 1A4, www.railtowncafe.ca).

31 Folkart Interiors
Wooden Mountie headquarters

What is it about the Royal Canadian Mounted Police (RCMP) uniform that makes it so instantly recognisable around the world? Is it the distinctive brown hat, the famous red serge, or the thin yellow stripe down the side of the trousers?

Dave Johnson, the owner of Folkart Interiors, has had a lot of time to think about it. For over 30 years, he has sold hundreds of life-sized, wooden Mountie statues from the corner of 10th and Alma. They can be seen standing on guard everywhere from trendy Whistler apartments to Gastown shops. He has even shipped them overseas to expats craving a bit of Canadiana in places as far-flung as Australia and Dubai. Once, years ago, the store was commissioned to create a 25-foot wooden Mountie for the entrance to the Coast High Country Inn in the Yukon, a territory where Mounties certainly feel at home. That Mountie stands there to this day and has become a real tourist attraction in Whitehorse.

On a more practical note, he also sells ornamental six-inch ones too, but it is the big, six-foot-tall ones for which he is most famous. They are all hand-carved by local artists, but don't worry – no trees are killed in the making of these Mounties. All of the carvings at Folkart Interiors are from British Columbia windfall trees that were blown over naturally in storms. That's not to say his Mounties are a pushover; the nine-footer standing outside the store keeps the place safe.

Once you make it past that Mountie, you'll find a fantastic selection of other Canadian antique collectibles and handmade local furniture. Give yourself plenty of time in the store to browse through the antique birdcages, old slot machines, blankets, boxes, and hundreds of other curios, including paintings of Mounties.

If bringing home a 'timbered' version of Dudley Do-Right of the RCMP isn't your style, Folkart can custom carve a figure of your pet from a photo.

Address 3720 West 10th Avenue, Vancouver, BC V6R 2G4, +1 (604) 731-7576,
www.folkartinteriors.com | Getting there By car, metered parking is available on West
10th Avenue | Hours Tue–Sat 11am–5pm, Sun noon–5pm | Tip Actual RCMP
Officers still keep the peace across most of Canada. If you want to see what a typical
local RCMP detachment looks like, there's one not far from Folkart Interiors on the
UBC Campus (2290 Westbrook Mall, Vancouver, BC V6T 2B7).

32 Fortes' Fountain
Font of gratitude

When it was placed in Alexandra Park nearly a century ago, this public drinking fountain was – like Joe Fortes himself – a handsome and practical addition to the local scene. Today, Alexandra Park is a shadow of its old self, and Joe's fountain is literally in the shadows (though still handsome). Even so, it's worth stopping by to check out this often overlooked memorial to one of Vancouver's earliest and best-loved residents.

Joe's legacy as the city's first official lifeguard and swimming teacher is well known by Vancouverites. He saved many dozens of swimmers from drowning and was an omnipresent feature in English Bay, where he camped out overnight in the summer months.

Fewer people know that this fountain, located a stone's throw away from where Joe's cottage on Bidwell Street used to be, was created by Austrian immigrant Charles Marega (1871–1939). That's the same person who designed the iconic lions that stand as sentinels at Lions Gate Bridge, the statue of George Vancouver outside City Hall, 14 sculptures around the exterior of the Legislative Library of British Columbia in Victoria, and a bust of Benito Mussolini that was retrieved from the basement of the former Italian Consulate after World War II and anonymously donated to the Vancouver archives. Marega also created the nine nude muses supporting the cornice of the Beaux Arts-style Sun Tower building at 128 West Pender Street.

This memorial fountain was installed in 1927, five years after nearly everyone in Vancouver attended the public funeral put on for Fortes by the city. The public raised the funds to build the memorial. He was honoured again in 2013, when Canada Post put his image on two million postage stamps. So as you stand here and admire the memorial that says, *Children loved him*, remember a time when the city was in its own infancy, and when neighbours were heroes.

Address Alexandra Park, 1755 Beach Avenue, Vancouver, BC V6E 1V3,
+1 (604) 873-7000 | Getting there By car, residential street parking is available nearby |
Hours Unrestricted | Tip Vancouver's majestic Inukshuk at English Bay, inspiration for the
Vancouver 2010 Olympic logo, is just across the street. The Inukshuk was created by Alvin
Kanak, sponsored by the Government of the Northwest Territories for its Expo 86 pavilion
and subsequently gifted to the City of Vancouver (1700 Beach Avenue, Vancouver,
BC V6E 1V3, www.stanleyparkvan.com/stanley-park-van-monument-inukshuk.html).

33__ Gaoler's Mews
A place to hang

Prior to the great fire of 1886, Gaoler's Mews was where a jail and the hangman's gallows were located. This was definitely a place you'd not want to be seen hanging around. But today, it's the location of No. 1 Gaoler's Mews, a place where gourmet enthusiasts eagerly await the opportunity to be served an exclusive, 10-course meal prepared only once a month by some of the top chefs in the city. If you're hanging out here now, you've probably done something right.

The name of the place tells the story of its origins. A mews was created here in the mid-1800s to stable horses for the carriage company running the route between Burrard inlet and New Westminster. When the jail ('gaol') came along, the mews became Gaoler's Mews. The Mews is a courtyard surrounded by Water Street on the north side, Carrall on the east, and Trounce Alley on the south side. Many refer to the alley as 'Blood Alley' because it helps make the area seem spooky. But Blood Alley is really just the cobbled courtyard area – Blood Alley Square – between the mews and Cordova Street. The confusion over the name and history of the area owes much to the savvy marketers of the 1970s who were eager to turn the dilapidated and hippy-infested Gastown area into a must-see place for tourists and thrill-seekers. They were also keen to avoid the alternative plan, which was to tear down all the historic buildings and put in a spanking new freeway. So tales of hangings, mass executions, ghost sightings, and bloody alleys were part of the plan to draw business to the area. Gastown's old-timey Steam Clock entered the scene in the 1970s too.

Despite the gloss of ghoulish marketing, Gaoler's Mews is a legitimately historic and interesting place to visit. If all you have ever seen of Gastown are the main streets, you owe it to yourself to duck down into Gaoler's Mews and hang out for a bit. But bring a friend – you never know who (or what) may be lurking there.

Address 12 Water Street, Vancouver, BC V6B 1A5 | Getting there By car, forget about street parking; closest parking lots are at 160 Water Street, or at 312 Abbott Street | Hours Unrestricted | Tip Just around the corner is Maple Leaf Square, one of the most historic intersections in Vancouver and the place where the Gassy Jack statue was toppled by demonstrators in 2022 (1 Water Street, Vancouver, BC V6B 2H9, www.heritagesitefinder.ca/location/maple-tree-square).

34 Giant Metal Haida Crab

Most photographed crab in Canada

There is no way to prove definitively that this crab is the most photographed one in Canada, but there's no denying that it is quite photogenic. While it seems like it was built yesterday, the 20-foot-tall steel crustacean was actually made 50 years ago. Designed by artist George Norris, the sculpture's genesis extends back to Canada's centennial celebrations in 1967 that spawned many infrastructure and artistic endeavours across the city. In fact, the building behind the crab was also a centennial project, officially dedicated on May 20, 1967 by Queen Elizabeth's cousin, Princess Alexandra.

The crab was created with the help of Gus Lidberg, who spent three months welding the pieces together in a studio on Main Street, near today's Olympic Village, before it was transported here by barge. Just imagine if it had fallen off the barge … there'd be a really big metal crab lurking at the bottom of False Creek. It was officially installed on October 14, 1968 and is perhaps one of the best examples of public art that has aged well. At an original cost of $20,000, this crab is quite a bargain.

Norris preferred not to name any of his works, so you can call the crab whatever you want. Many call it the Haida Crab because Norris was supposedly inspired by a Haida First Nations' legend, in which the crab is a creature that guards the entrance to a harbour. But some people just call it "that big, metal crab."

The building behind the crab, which looks to some like a flying saucer, was designed by architect Gerald Hamilton to reflect the shape of the conical traditional headwear worn by the Northwest Coast First Nations People. Most people think of this building as the planetarium or space centre, but it was initially intended as a permanent home for the Centennial Museum, now operating as the Museum of Vancouver, which actually uses the majority of the space.

Address 1100 Chestnut Street, Vancouver, BC V6J 3J9, www.museumofvancouver.ca, guestservices@museumofvancouver.ca | Getting there By car, paid parking is available at the Museum of Vancouver/HR MacMillan Space Centre | Hours Unrestricted | Tip The home of Vancouver's first official city archivist, Major J. S. Matthews, is a short walk away (1343 Maple Street, Vancouver, BC V6J 3S1). Built in 1911, it is one of the earliest homes in the neighbourhood and was for a time the focal point of much of Vancouver's earliest historical records and archives.

35 Granville Island Silos
Big art from Brazil

Whoever made those concrete silos on Granville Island probably never imagined that one day they would become the canvas for one of the largest displays of public art in Canada. But that's exactly what happened. The four silos, all still in full use, were turned into a 23,000-square-foot, 360-degree work of art in 2014 by Brazilian twin brothers Octavio and Gustavo Pandolfo as part of a public art program initiated by a non-profit charitable organisation, Vancouver Biennale.

The 70-foot-tall mural features six characters created in the unique style that has made the Pandolfo brothers among the top graffiti and street artists in the world. Two of the six face out towards the water while the other four face in toward the land. One wears a hoodie and a mask. Two are brown-skinned and four are Simpsons-yellow. When completed, the six giants were the largest works created by the Pandolfo brothers, who go by the professional moniker of OSGEMEOS (which is Portuguese for 'The Twins'). Some of their other works have covered buildings in San Francisco, New York, Mumbai, Berlin, Milan, the Tate Gallery in London, and even a 737 jet as part of the 2014 FIFA World Cup in Brazil. The spray-can sporting siblings have even collaborated with Louis Vuitton on the design of a scarf. All of their colourful creations share the same mix of Brazilian culture and hip-hop style that has become their trademark. The formal name for the silos art installation is *Giants*.

The silos are still actively used by the Ocean Concrete Company, which has been operating on Granville Island since 1920 and produces unknown tonnes of concrete each year. Some of the cement goes to and from the plant in their brightly wrapped, ready-mix truck drums, and some is shipped out by barge. Their cement has been used in many buildings in Vancouver, most notably the Vancouver Public Library.

Address 1415 Johnson Street, Granville Island, Vancouver, BC V6H 3R9, www.osgemeos.com.br/en | Getting there By ferry, Granville Island Ferry Dock; by car, closest paid parking is the Anderson Street parking lot at 1402 Anderson Street | Hours Unrestricted | Tip The Vancouver Mural Festival is the city's largest annual free public art celebration. Find out how to take the tour or check out their extensive online mural map at www.vanmuralfest.ca.

36 Greenpeace Plaque
Where the activists first made waves

Today, Greenpeace is a well-funded international non-governmental organisation, well-known in Vancouver and around the world for environmental activism. But back in 1971, they were an ill-defined proto-organisation determined to stop the US military from testing a nuclear bomb in the Bering Sea. In fact, they weren't even called Greenpeace yet. They were called the Don't Make a Wave Committee because they thought that exploding a nuclear bomb off the Alaskan island of Amchitka would create a devastating tsunami and trigger earthquakes.

Following the philosophy of passive resistance, their stop-the-nukes strategy was to halt the bomb testing by 'bearing witness' to the event. In other words, they aimed to show up at the test zone. But getting from Vancouver to Amchitka, 4,000 kilometres away on the western end of the Aleutian Islands, was easier said than done. The passionate peaceniks decided the best way to bear witness was to hire a boat and sail it up there. So they organised a concert at the Pacific Coliseum, featuring Joni Mitchell, James Taylor, Phil Ochs, and newly-formed Canadian rock band, Chilliwack. With the $18,000 they made from that event, they chartered a halibut seiner called the *Phyllis Cormack*. Renaming her *Greenpeace*, the crew of 12 set sail for Alaska from near this point on False Creek on September 15, 1971.

As it happens, the test was delayed before they were able to put themselves in harm's way. On the face of it, the mission was a failure. But the press clippings were sensational, and the name of the ship was the talk of the town. As word of the mission continued to spread, so to did interest in the organising committee, and a year later the Don't Make A Wave Committee did the savvy thing and changed their name to Greenpeace. The rest is history. As for the *Phyllis Cormack*, she sunk in deep water off Klemtu in 1998.

Address 1500 Island Park Walk, Vancouver, BC V6J 5B3, www.greenpeace.org/canada/en | Getting there By car, closest paid parking is the Impark lot at 1585 West 2nd Avenue; by ferry, closest dock is Granville Island dock | Hours Unrestricted | Tip If the weather is fine, grab a seat on the deck at nearby Go Fish seafood shack (1501 West 1st Avenue, Vancouver, BC V6J 1E8) and enjoy some fish and chips!

37 Gulf of Georgia Cannery
You'll be hooked

Visit the working fishing community of Steveston in Richmond, and you are never far from the mouthwatering smell of a fresh batch of fish and chips emanating from the fryer in one of the many great seafood restaurants. But a hundred years ago, the same streets were plagued with a terrible stench coming from the fish cannery down the street.

Today that old, massive, red and white wooden cannery building is still perched on sturdy barnacle covered pylons at the exact same spot where it was built in 1894. Standing on the original receiving dock looking out across the Fraser River, you can imagine the mountains of fish that came off of an endless flotilla of boats that unloaded there. But you don't have to imagine how each and every one of those fish was processed and canned because you can just go inside and see for yourself the intact heavy industrial equipment that used to do the job. The work inside was hard, wet, smelly, and dangerous for the hundreds of ethnically diverse Chinese, Japanese, First Nations, and European workers that toiled endlessly to pack away up to 2.5 million cans of salmon a year. One of the noisy processing machines had a long moving track with a huge rotating blade that would cut each salmon's head off, and then the fish moved further down the line to be pinned under a wheel that chopped off its fins and tail. Their bellies were opened with a saw and then… well you will just have to visit this National Historic Site to fully understand.

On a less gross note, the cannery also features a big wall display where you can discover the different species of fish that live in the waters off Canada's West Coast. Enthusiastic docents dressed in traditional cannery worker clothing give wonderful guided tours. And don't worry – all the machines have been thoroughly cleaned and are totally devoid of that old fishy smell.

Address 12138 4th Avenue, Richmond, BC V7E 3J1, +1 (604) 664-9009, www.gulfofgeorgiacannery.org, info@gogcannery.org | Getting there By car, paid parking is available on site at Chatham Street and 4th Avenue | Hours Daily 10am–5pm | Tip Steveston is famous for its fish and chips and you'll find about half a dozen restaurants there that sell the West Coast staple dish. The best one is Dave's Fish and Chips, which has been there since 1978. It's not far from the cannery (3460 Moncton Street, BC V7E 3A2, www.davesfishandchips.com).

38 __ H Tasting Lounge

Howard Hughes slept here – for a long, long time

Imagine you are the hotel manager working the front desk at the Bayshore Inn in 1972, when the phone rings. It's a call from billionaire aviator and Hollywood movie producer Howard Hughes. At the time, he was on the run for tax evasion and needed a place to hide after his trail had taken him from London to the Bahamas, and then Panama. He requested to book into the Bayshore Inn (as it was known then) for six months. Here is where, like Howard Hughes himself, it gets weird. He asked to take over the entire top four floors of the hotel. The manager politely had to tell Mr. Hughes, "I am sorry, we are full." Hughes responded, "If I don't get the rooms, I'm buying the hotel." From anyone else, that condescending statement would have been dismissed as nothing more than an idle threat. However, the threat had precedence because years before, when Hughes had been asked to check out of the Desert Inn, instead of leaving he bought the Las Vegas Landmark.

And so began one of the most bizarre chapters in Vancouver hotel history. Hughes was 66 years old at the time and one of the most famous men alive. Everywhere the strange recluse travelled to was big international news, and the paparazzi camped out in front of the Bayshore for his entire six-month stay. To ensure security, the elevator to the top four floors was blocked off, and the bathrobed hermit used the housekeeping elevator to move around.

Hughes is long gone, but the memory of his stay has been captured in a new bar in the hotel. It's called the H Tasting Lounge. As you would expect, it has an aviation theme; the stunning chandelier is formed out of small, spiralling, crystal propellers, and the décor is art deco in pastel hues of blue and pink that were popular during his stay.

If you run into a scruffy senior while you are at the bar, please escort him back to the freight elevator.

Address 1601 Bayshore Drive, Vancouver, BC V6G 2V4, +1 (604) 682-3377, www.htastinglounge.com, info@htastinglounge.com | Getting there By car, metered parking is available on Cardero and paid parking is available at the hotel | Hours Daily 11:30am – midnight | Tip Near the Westin Bayshore is a great spot to rent a bike and then disembark for a scenic ride along the Stanley Park Seawall. Spokes Bicycle Rentals has been serving the citizens and tourists of Vancouver since 1938 (1798 West Georgia Street, Vancouver, BC V6G 2V7, www.spokesbicyclerentals.com).

39__The Haida Canoe
Cedar icon at UBC

If there were a top ten list of iconic Canadian watercraft, the Haida Canoe would surely be on it. Most Canadians recognize it from the old 20-dollar bill, which featured Bill Reid's famous sculpture, *Spirit of Haida Gwaii* – the original sculpture rests grandly at the Canadian Embassy in Washington, DC, while its twin version, *The Jade Canoe* wows international visitors at the Vancouver airport. The Haida Canoe is a well-known and much-loved Canadian symbol today, but this was not always the case.

When early explorers visited Vancouver's waters, there were thousands of craft like this – some 600 of them surrounded the trading vessel of Captain Thomas Barnett in 1791. But a century later, very few were still in use. By the early 20th century, it was hard to find anyone who still knew how to make one. Credit for their revival belongs to artist Bill Reid who, together with other Haida artists, carved one from a single red cedar log for the Vancouver Expo in 1986.

This northern canoe was used by the Haida, Tsimshian, and Tlingit people living between Northern Vancouver Island and southern Alaska and was designed for long ocean journeys. They could be small enough for one person or big enough to carry five tonnes of cargo.

Reid's 1986 version was called *Loo Taas* ('wave eater'). This one at UBC is called *The Looplex X* and is suspended 40 feet above the ground in the foyer of the Forestry building. The location is no accident for, apart from its beauty and cultural symbolism, the canoe inspires forestry students to consider how a single tree can provide material for construction of so many things. The outer bark, inner bark, and roots of this lightweight and strong wood with straight grain and few knots, were all used to the great benefit of the indigenous peoples. Its story is inspiring to anyone who chooses to remember and learn from the past.

Address 2424 Main Mall, Vancouver, BC V6T 1Z4, +1 (604) 822-2727,
www.infrastructuredevelopment.ubc.ca/projects/forest-sciences-centre-haida-looplex-x |
Getting there By car, closest parking lot is the UBC Thunderbird Parkade at 6085 Thunder-
bird Boulevard | Hours See website visitor information | Tip The Reconciliation Totem
Pole, also made from a single western red cedar tree, is located just outside the Forestry
building and tells the history of indigenous people in Canada before, during, and after the
Indian residential school era.

40 Hamilton's Missing Plaque

Vancouver's first street corner

On a winter day in 1885, at the corner of Hastings and Hamilton Streets, Lauchlan Alexander Hamilton "stood in the silent solitude of the primeval forest" and drove a wooden stake into the earth. With that act completed, Vancouver's first land commissioner and Canadian Pacific Rail surveyor set about his job of surveying the land and creating the first street grid for the city. He not only determined where the streets would go, he also named many of them. In the West End, he used names of British Admirals (Nelson, Denman, Burrard). In Fairview, he used tree names (Alder, Birch, Cedar). Some streets were named after battles (Balaclava, Blenheim, Waterloo).

Almost 70 years later on April 20, 1953, a bronze plaque, designed by English sculptor Sydney March and dedicated by Vancouver's first archivist J. S. Matthews, was created to honour Hamilton and commemorate his singular act that established Vancouver's first street corner. The plaque was unveiled at a dinner attended by everyone who had moved to Vancouver prior to the arrival of the first passenger train in 1887 (see ch. 65) and was then mounted on the exterior wall of the stately Canadian Imperial Bank of Commerce building that occupied this remarkable site next to Victory Square. Generations of Vancouverites grew accustomed to passing by the unobtrusive plaque on their way to work or just going about their business until, another 70 years later, the CIBC building was torn down. In its place now stands Simon Fraser University's spanking new Charles Chang Innovation Centre, a graduate student residence and innovation facility. There was some vague talk during construction that the Hamilton plaque would be reinstalled in the foyer of the new building, but so far it remains secured out of sight. It may one day become viewable again but, in the meantime, maybe there should be a plaque here saying there used to be a plaque here?

Address Corner of Hastings Street and Hamilton Street, Vancouver, BC V6B 2N4 | Getting there By car, metered parking is available nearby | Hours Unrestricted | Tip Enjoy some of the best Lebanese food in town at nearby Nuba in Gastown, located below street level in the historic Dominion building, once the tallest commercial building in the British Empire (207 West Hastings Street, Vancouver, BC V6B 1K6, www.nuba.ca).

41 Harbour Air

Have you ever seen a flying beaver?

Floatplanes with romantic model names like the Flying Beaver literally opened the Canadian North during the 1940s and 1950s. Adventurous tales of explorers, miners, missionaries, and trappers pioneering Canada's rugged wilderness in water landing planes are legendary.

Although the swashbuckling Bush Pilots of yesterday are becoming a rare breed, the style of planes they commandeered are still around, and nowhere in the world are they more easily viewed in action than in the heart of downtown Vancouver's Coal Harbour. That is where you will find Harbour Air, a company that runs the largest all-seaplane airline in the world.

At Harbour Air's dock, you are sure to see plenty of floatplanes moored. Although there is no real runway in the traditional paved sense, the patch of water on Coal Harbour has dozens of scheduled passenger flights landing and taking off from it every day. It is amazing to watch these small floatplanes with their buoyant pontoons splash down and land in this high-traffic, maritime transportation hub. The floatplanes that leave the harbour fly all over the Gulf Islands, the Sunshine Coast, and up to Whistler, but their main destination is the Victoria Inner Harbour. As a matter of fact, that harbour-to-harbour service is one of the busiest air routes in Canada.

With all those planes coming and going, someone has to keep track of and traffic them. The Vancouver Harbour Control tower situated on top of a Vancouver office building overlooking the harbour is the tallest air traffic control tower in the world, reaching 466 feet above the ground.

The only thing more fun than watching the planes take off and land is being inside of one of them when they do. You can, of course, buy a ticket to go to one of Harbour Air's scheduled destinations, or, if you wish, maybe even charter your own flight to take you up north into the backcountry.

Address 1979–2155 Stanley Park Drive, Vancouver, BC V6G 3E2 | Getting there
By car, paid parking lot behind the statue near the Totem Poles | Hours Unrestricted |
Tip If the statue and story inspire you to go for a run then Just Do It. At the entrance to
Stanley Park you will find a well-stocked running shoe store called the Running Room
(679 Denman Street, Suite 203, Vancouver, BC V6G 2L3, www.runningroom.com/ca).

44 Hastings Mill Store Museum

Vancouver's oldest building

An odd feature of Vancouver's oldest building, a survivor of the great fire of 1886 that burned the early city to the ground, is that it is not in its original location. It used to be on the north end of Dunlevy Avenue, in the neighbourhood we now call Railtown, but was moved to the more bucolic Point Grey location by barge in 1931 in order to save it a second time (this time, from the developers' wrecking ball). What survives inside the building is as amazing as the structure itself: the original table used by the first Vancouver City Council, Joe Fortes' oil lamp (see ch. 32), artefacts from the storied SS *Beaver* (see ch. 96), and hundreds of curios from the earliest days when Vancouver was a small lumber town at the edge of the sprawling British Empire.

The store began life in the late 1860s as an annex to Stamp's Mill, a lumber mill started by Captain Edward Stamp. Like many entrepreneurial enterprises, the first few years were rocky. The business went under new management and was rebranded as the Hastings Mill in 1870. Regardless, the mill store was always the go-to place for the city's earliest labourers to get their supplies, the Amazon of its day, providing everything from pipe tobacco to underwear.

The lumber mill and the mill store were the centre of economic and social enterprise for the quickly developing city of Vancouver and is the indisputable ground zero for the economic development of the city. At least, that was the case until the CPR put the railway station at the end of Granville Street in 1886 and shifted the momentum westward. By 1928, the mill was ready to be torn down, and it was only thanks to a local women's group that the store was saved. It seems a pity the building had to be moved far away from the context in which it once thrived, but few can doubt that moving it is what saved it so we can still enjoy it today.

Address 1575 Alma Street, Vancouver, BC V6R 3P3, +1 (604) 734-1212, www.hastingsmillmuseum.ca, hastings.mill@gmail.com | Getting there By car, free street parking is available nearby | Hours See website for seasonal hours | Tip Not far from the Hastings Mill Store, down a well-aged cement staircase at the end of Cameron Avenue, is a place where you can enjoy a spectacular Vancouver sunset as the water laps at your feet below (Cameron Avenue, Vancouver, BC V6R 3P3).

45 Hendrix's Grandma's House

And the wind cries Nora

Most people know that musical phenomenon Jimi Hendrix was from Seattle and that he died far too young. Not many know that his grandmother Zenora 'Nora' Rose Hendrix resided in Vancouver, where she lived to the distinguished age of 100. Nora was a pillar of the African-Canadian community, which was centred around the area of Strathcona at Main and Union Streets during the 1920s. She was the co-founder of Vancouver's first Black church, the Fountain Chapel, which was the local institution within the African Methodist Episcopal (AME) Church and welcomed many of its pastors into her home.

Nora was born in Tennessee and was part of a travelling vaudeville group. She ended up settling in Vancouver in 1911 after marrying Ross Hendrix. They had three children. Al, the youngest, was born in 1919. He moved to Seattle at the age of 22, where he met Lucille, and they had a son named James 'Jimi' Marshall Hendrix in 1942.

Jimi spent summers in Vancouver at his grandmother's house until 1952. Those summers must have had a tremendous influence on the young musician. Nora worked as a cook at Vie's Chicken and Steak House, where she served the superstars, including Nat King Cole, Lena Horne, Billie Holiday, Ella Fitzgerald, Louis Armstrong, Sammy Davis Jr., and Duke Ellington. The Fountain Chapel was also an important gathering place for gospel singers.

In his youth, Jimi busked on Granville Street from time to time and performed at two well-known local night clubs: Dante's Inferno and the Smilin' Buddha, where he was fired for playing too loudly.

Nora passed away in 1984 and is buried in Renton, Washington, just outside of Seattle. But she was at the Pacific Coliseum on September 7, 1968 to watch her grandson perform on stage in The Jimi Hendrix Experience, one of the hottest bands of the time.

Address 827 East Georgia Street, Vancouver, BC V6A 2A5 | Getting there By car, street parking is available | Hours Unrestricted from the outside only | Tip Continue your tour of Jimi Hendrix's early life to the place where Vie's Chicken and Steak House once stood. There you will find a blue brick building where Jimi used to practise his guitar after hours (209 Union Street, Vancouver, BC V6A 2V7).

46 Heritage Harbour

Tall stories and masts from the past

This area used to be a rather quaint little harbour with a collection of old boats that looked as though they had seen better days and had come here to retire ... or sink. But today, there's a fresh wind filling the sails of wooden boat enthusiasts with new hope and new energy. Heritage Harbour now hosts only those boats that are historically significant and have a tall tale to tell. All but two of the boats are privately owned, and all of the owners need to give the harbour master, Bruce MacDonald, a good sales pitch if they want to dock there. Being old or pretty (the boat) isn't good enough. Bruce's boat, The *North Star of Herschel Island*, has set a high standard. The Arctic icon, built in 1935, was a familiar name among many chronologers of Canadian adventure, including authors Pierre Berton and Farley Mowat.

Other ships on display in the harbour include *The Mysterion*, built in 1927 using wood salvaged from *The Empress of Japan*. *The Sylvester* is a 19.6-foot-long, flat-bottomed boat in the 'dory' style and was once owned by Will Millar of the Irish Rovers. On permanent display is the RCMP ship *Nadon*, which circumnavigated North America by taking the Northwest Passage to the East Coast and coming back via the Panama Canal. The harbour is a bit of a moving feast, and you'll never know exactly what ships will be there when you arrive, which makes it all the more interesting.

An exciting new development is the plan by Simon Fawkes and Danny Robertson, owners of *The Providence*, an 80-foot Gaff Ketch built in 1903, to make environmentally-friendly trading voyages to the Gulf Islands, returning on weekends to sell fresh island produce directly from the ship. In the winter months they might even sail down to South America on a coffee run. So weigh anchor and sail on over to Heritage Harbour for an experience that promises to delight the eyes and fuel the imagination.

Address 1905 Ogden Avenue, Vancouver, BC V6J 1A3, www.vancouvermaritimemuseum.com | Getting there By car, the closest paid parking is at 900 Chestnut Street; by ferry, to Maritime Museum | Hours Daily dawn–dusk | Tip Walk toward the A-frame Maritime Museum building, and you'll soon see the *Ben Franklin* submarine who's crew of six explorers drifted 2,300 kilometres (1,444 miles) through the Gulf Stream over 30 days in 1969.

47___Hidden Seawall Symbols

A treasure hunt carved into the stones

Vancouver's crown jewel attraction is the Stanley Park Seawall. Much has been written about it over the past 100 years, but there is a special secret about the stones in the wall that you won't find on the Internet, and up until the publication of this book almost no one knew about. It's a hidden gem that will finally be revealed in the last paragraph.

Most of the seawall was built between 1917 and 1971 under the supervision of a master stonemason named James Cunningham. He spent 35 years of his life carefully fitting together the hundreds of thousands of rocks that form the protective barrier to the sea. You can't help but admire the way they all fit together as you loop your way around the stunning marine pathway. However, after a while all the rocks start to look the same.

That is until you get to Third Beach and it turns into a bit of a treasure hunt. Just follow these hush-hush instructions. At Third Beach, there is a set of stairs leading down from the concession stand to the seawall. Use the bottom of those stairs as your starting point and walk 100 paces south. You will know that you are walking in the right direction (south) if the ocean is on your right. The four-foot-wide rock divider between the bike path and the walking path will be on your left and that's the side on which your search will focus. Once you have hit 100 paces, look carefully over the stones in the divider. You'll discover some carefully chiseled rock shapes that may tell you something about James Cunningham.

Was he a hockey fan, a card player, or just a proud Canadian? He was probably all three. If you carefully study the divider where you are standing, you'll see stones in the shape of a hockey puck and hockey stick. You'll see stones in the shape of the four card suits (hearts, spades, clubs, diamonds), and finally, you will see a stone carved into a maple leaf.

Address Stanley Park Causeway, Vancouver, BC V6G 1Z4, www.vancouver.ca/parks-recreation-culture/stanley-park.aspx | Getting there By car, paid parking available at the Third Beach concession lot off Stanley Drive | Hours Unrestricted | Tip After he died, James Cunningham's ashes were buried behind Siwash Rock, and if you're resourceful you can find the plaque with his name there. Siwash Rock is located just over half a kilometre (third of a mile) further north along the seawall path. Best to go at low tide.

48 Holy Rosary Cathedral

Where Frankenstein's Bride was married

Long before he became the star of Hollywood's iconic 1935 horror movie *Bride of Frankenstein*, Boris Karloff (real name William Pratt) married the first of his six wives, Grace Harding, at Holy Rosary Cathedral on February 2, 1910. She would have been horrified to think that one day she might jokingly be referred to as the 'original bride of Frankenstein', but, then again, considering the marriage only lasted three years, maybe she would have agreed after all.

In any case, it's interesting to stand at the entrance of the cathedral and contemplate the many people and changes this building has seen over its rich history. The building dates back to a wooden church built here in 1886, and ever since the church has been a reflection of Vancouver and its times. The funeral for Joe Fortes (see ch. 32) took place here in 1922 following the largest procession the city had ever seen. In the 1950s, the Holy Rosary's Father J. E. Brown came under the influence of Alfred M. Hubbard ('the Johnny Appleseed of LSD') and dropped acid while praising the spiritual potential of psychedelics to parishioners. In 1981, Chief Dan George of the Tsleil-Waututh Nation and star of many Hollywood westerns, had his funeral here, and Pope John Paul II walked through these doors in 1984.

Celebrity history aside, visitors to the cathedral today respectfully marvel at a number of artistic treasures resting among the Norman columns of red scagliola marble, which support the gothic tunnel vault. These include the oldest romantic-style pipe organ in the province, and 21 glorious stained-glass windows. Of particular note are the five Guido Nincheri windows completed about 60 years ago. The window showing Our Lady of the Holy Rosary was once featured on a Canada Post Christmas stamp. Not to be missed, outside the church, is the stunning contemporary sculpture of *Homeless Jesus* by Canadian artist Timothy Schmalz.

Address 646 Richards Street, Vancouver, BC V6B 3A3, +1 (604) 682-6747, www.holyrosarycathedral.org, office@vancouvercathedral.org | Getting there SkyTrain to Granville or Stadium-Chinatown (Expo Line); by car, Impark lot no. 1037 is closest and metered parking is available on Richard Street | Hours See website for visitor information | Tip Christ Church Cathedral is about half a kilometre away (690 Burrard Street, Vancouver, BC V6C 3L1, www.thecathedral.ca) and worth visiting to see the Repository for Regimental Colours located in the east chancel alcove. When you do, you'll be walking in the footsteps of Prince Charles and Diana, Princess of Wales, who worshipped here in 1986.

49 Honeybee Centre
Un-bee-lievable

If honeybees ever become extinct, we are all in a lot of trouble. They pollinate about a third of what we eat. A lot of Vancouverites support, nurture, and study these fascinating little creatures in a province sometimes referred to as 'Bee-Cee'. Commercial and hobby beekeepers' hives can be found in abundance in fields, backyards, and on the roofs of downtown buildings. In 2003, the City of Vancouver made residential beekeeping legal. Now, altogether there are over 2,300 registered beekeepers in the province who tend to over 45,000 colonies. Each colony consists of about 20,000 to 30,000 bees. You do the math.

The Honeybee Centre is a very special place that provides educational resources, sells honey and other bee byproducts, and even has a live indoor hive on display. The Honeybee Centre is about 30 kilometres from Vancouver in the municipality of Surrey, a bit further out in the country, where there's a lot of good foraging for the bees. While you are shopping there, keep in mind that honeybees on average can fly up to a range of about five kilometres, and the entire hive gathers the nectar from over two million flowers and plants to make just one of those one-pound jars on the shelf. The honey they sell comes from a wide variety of plants, including buckwheat, blueberry, fireweed, and clover. They each have distinct flavours.

Founded in 2002, the centre's mission is to enrich the lives of people through the mysterious and incredible world of the honeybee. The large retail operation is the heart of the centre, while a barn and a few other outbuildings make up the rest of the complex. A restaurant attached to the store is appropriately called the Beestro. It serves delicious artisan salads, baked goods, and tasty treats, many of which, of course, contain the delicious golden elixir. Although lots of animals, including humans, can eat insects, did you know that bees are the only insect that create food that humans can eat?

Address 7480 176 Street, Surrey, BC V3S 7B1, +1 (604) 575-2337, www.honeybeecentre.com |
Hours Daily 10am–6pm | Tip The Honeybee Centre has a smaller retail location, the Main
Street Honey Shoppe, in the heart of Vancouver (4125 Main Street Vancouver, BC V5V 3P6).

50 Hotel Georgia

Classiest joint in town

Some buildings have their heyday and then fade into mere echoes of their glorious past. Others start life as unspectacular and acquire fame over time. Neither is the case with the Hotel Georgia, however. This gem has always been on the 'A' list. If this is one of those places you've walked past a million times and never stopped in to visit, then now is the time to fix that oversight. You don't need to book a room – just walk right in. The bar in the lobby lounge serves classic cocktails from the golden age of jazz that will knock your socks off. While enjoying your cocktail, relax in the classy lounge area and take in some of the photographs of this stately landmark's past visitors: Elvis, The Beatles, Louis Armstrong, Nat King Cole, Queen Elizabeth, and John Wayne to name a few.

Opened in 1927, the hotel soon became the bee's knees of the jazz and big band society – so much so that British Columbia's most popular radio station, CKWX, moved in permanently and broadcast 'live' from the top floor.

The hotel was very nearly the place of Errol Flynn's last days. The swashbuckling swordsman was a registered guest when visiting Vancouver with his teenage girlfriend in 1959. But it turns out, he spent most of his time swilling down the giggle water at cocktail parties, and it's not clear if he ever actually checked in. The only thing known for sure is that he – and his liver – checked out permanently at a party on 1310 Burnaby Street in Vancouver.

Although the $120-million renovation completed in 2011 reduced the number of rooms from 313 to 155, many of the designated heritage property aspects were retained. An official cultural heritage site in Canada, and located close to everything downtown, it's worthwhile to stop in, if only for a moment, to look around and wonder what it must have been like when Marlene Dietrich showed up with her 40 suitcases.

Address 801 West Georgia Street, Vancouver, BC V6C 1P7, +1 (604) 682-5566, www.rosewoodhotels.com/en/hotel-georgia-vancouver | Getting there SkyTrain to Vancouver City Centre (Canada Line); by car, metered parking is available nearby | Hours See website for bar and restaurant hours | Tip The Bill Reid Gallery of Northwest Coast Art is located just around the corner (639 Hornby Street, Vancouver, BC V6C 2G3, www.billreidgallery.ca). The Gallery is home to the Simon Fraser University Bill Reid Collection and special exhibitions of contemporary indigenous art of the Northwest Coast of North America.

51 Houdini's Great Escape

Where the magician once hung out – literally

"Over this spot, on March 1, 1923, the world's greatest escapologist Harry Houdini cheated death and captured the attention of the entire city," is what the brass marker on the pavement outside 137 West Pender Street *should* say. Regrettably, there is no marker. And the act, which stopped traffic nearly a century ago, remains only in the history books. But if you go to this rather nondescript place today, you can stand in the place that might very well have been the site of Houdini's death – had things gone wrong.

One might wonder why the president of the Society of American Magicians was hanging by his ankles outside a second-story window, wearing a straitjacket, and wrapped in chains at this location. The answer is that, in addition to being a master escapologist, Houdini was also a master promoter and entertainer. And what better way to draw attention to one's show at the Orpheum Theatre than a free publicity stunt hosted at the location of *The Vancouver Sun* newspaper? And with Mrs. Houdini looking on too. Pure marketing genius.

Houdini's show sold out, and he continued to perform similar stunts across North America and around the world. He survived many more death-defying feats and, like today's Penn and Teller act, had no qualms about exposing con artists, especially spiritual mediums. But he was unable to beat the effects of a ruptured appendicitis and died only three years after his Vancouver visit. Before he died, he promised his wife that he'd send a secret message from beyond the grave if such communication were possible. No word – yet. Some still conduct séances today in the hope that he'll make contact.

The Sun moved away from this location, and the original building was demolished. In its place stands the Pendera Building, a 113-unit, non-market housing building built in 1989. But the spirit of Houdini still hangs in the air.

Address 137 West Pender Street, Vancouver, BC V6B 1S4 | Getting there By car, metered street parking is available nearby | Hours Unrestricted | Tip Fans of the metaphysical might enjoy a tarot reading from The Good Spirit (309 Cambie Street, Vancouver, BC V6B 2N4, www.thegoodspirit.ca).

52 Huge Olympic Village Birds

Refurbished feathers

Where once stood the world's greatest Winter Olympic athletes now stand two big, refurbished birds. More specifically, one male and one female house sparrow, each approximately five metres tall. Three things make these giant, special sparrows even more interesting.

First, they were originally erected in Southeast False Creek Olympic Plaza, the site of the 2010 Olympic Winter Games Athletes' Village as part of City of Vancouver's Olympic and Paralympic Public Art Program, and they have been nesting there ever since. The 3,500-pound,16-foot-high winged creatures are the work of sculptor Myfanwy Macleod. Her inspiration was the 1963 Alfred Hitchcock classic horror movie *The Birds*.

Second, as young, growing families moved into the Athletes' Village condos, the birds inadvertently became an important recreational part of the community. The birds are made of an irresistible, slippery aluminum that toddlers loved to climb over and slide down. Older kids enjoyed skateboarding on them and riding their edges. During years and years of fun sparrow abuse, the damage done by all that skateboarding and sliding wore the birds down to the point where they had to be repaired, resulting in a $400,000 repair bill.

With the City of Vancouver's assistance, the two birds migrated. First, they flew the coop to Calgary for mould making and then were flown off to China for recasting in aluminum. They made it back to their False Creek home just in time for Vancouver Bird Week and the 2018 International Ornithological Congress.

When you see one of the giant, brown and white, shiny birds perched on either side of the courtyard near the False Creek waterfront, go ahead and take a sparrow selfie. Just please refrain from sliding or skateboarding down their backs.

Address Stanley Park, Vancouver, BC V6G 3E2, www.stanleyparkvan.com | **Getting there** By car, parking is available at the lot where Pipeline Road meets Rose Garden Lane or at the Aquarium | **Hours** Unrestricted | **Tip** The Japanese Hall and Vancouver Japanese Language School (487 Alexander Street, Vancouver, BC V6A 1C6, www.vjls-jh.com), built in 1928, is a great place to learn Japanese – and to learn more about the Japanese community in Vancouver.

55_Jericho Beach

From Jerry's Cove to hippie haven

When most people think of Jericho Beach, they think of the sailing club, the kayak and stand-up surfboard rental shop, or perhaps just a lovely place to picnic with friends. But this sleepy slice of coastal paradise has a very interesting past.

To begin with, there's the name of the place. If you thought it was named after the ancient city on the Jordan River, you'd be wrong. The prevailing theory is that Jericho is an iteration of the name of the lumber company located in the area in the late 1860s by Jeremiah ('Jerry') Rogers. If you say the name of his company, Jerry & Co, out loud a few times the theory seems to make sense. Jerry's lumber business faded away, and in the later part of the 1800s, the area had what was, at the time, Canada's first golf course west of Ontario.

In the 1920s, a flying boat station dominated the beach and was used for anti-smuggling operations, forestry patrols, transport to remote communities, and keeping an eye on overfishing from the United States. The RCAF took over the station in 1924, and soon Canadian Forces Base Jericho would be the largest military training base in Western Canada.

Today, the Sailing Centre, Arts Centre, and Youth Hostel buildings are all that remain of the military base. The hostel, formerly the NCO's barracks, entered Vancouver's cultural history as the scene of the Battle of Jericho on October 15, 1970. Hundreds of hippies occupying the place refused to follow eviction orders, so the city sent in the police – and lots of them. Newspaper accounts state that 250 riot police, 150 RCMP officers, a 9-man police motorcycle squad, and 8 military police were on the scene. The three-hour tousle also had guest appearances by Hare Krishna monks and members of the Jesus People's Army, and the Vancouver Liberation Front. Newspapers reported that "the smell of marijuana hung in the air." Some things never change.

Address 3941 Point Grey Road, Vancouver, BC V6R 1B5 | Getting there By car, paid parking is available at the Jericho Sailing Centre and at the Jericho Parking Lot | Hours Daily 6am–10pm | Tip The pub, located on the second floor of the Sailing Centre, is one of the best places to catch a summer sunset over Burrard Inlet. In mid-July, revive the hippy spirit and partake in the Vancouver Folk Festival (www.thefestival.bc.ca) in Jericho Beach Park.

56 Kitsilano Pool
Canada's longest swimming pool

This outdoor saltwater pool is quite possibly the single greatest architectural accomplishment in the city of Vancouver. It is beautiful to look at, offers stunning views of the mountains across the English Bay and Vancouver skyline, and is the perfect place to spend a sunny afternoon, or an entire day. Initially built in 1931 for what was then a considerable sum of $50,000 as part of a Depression-era job-creation project for the young city's quarter-million inhabitants, this public facility was instantly a treasure beyond measure and remains so to this day. The beach was named after Squamish Chief August Jack Khatsahlano when the streetcar line was installed in 1905.

Aside from its aesthetic qualities, the pool has impressive technical attributes. With swimming lanes measuring 137 metres (150 yards) long, it is nearly three times longer than an Olympic swimming pool. And the entire pool contains more than a million litres (a quarter-million gallons) of fresh seawater. It is also Vancouver's only *heated* saltwater pool.

But that is only half of the story. Go further back in time, and you'll discover that this beautiful stretch of beach was once known as Greer's Beach, part of a 200-acre parcel of land purchased for $200 by Sam Greer in 1884, 16 months before the city of Vancouver was incorporated. His plot ran from the water to 4th Avenue, and from roughly Balsam to Chestnut Street. Had he been able to keep the land, Greer's descendants would be sitting on a real estate empire worth hundreds of millions. But the province granted it to the Canadian Pacific Railway in 1885. An Irish-born veteran of the US Civil War, Greer didn't take it lightly. When the authorities tried to remove him from the property, he took his shotgun out and fired a load through the farmhouse door. The sheriff and deputy survived, but Greer eventually did have to leave.

Address Corner of Russ Baker Way and Airport Road, Richmond, BC V7B 1C4,
+1 (604) 207-7077 | Getting there By car, free parking in lot in front of the monument |
Hours Unrestricted | Tip Across the street from the park is a 40,000-square-foot, glass
airplane hangar with a clear view of a retired West Jet airliner and half a dozen other
smaller planes. The modern building is actually the heart of the British Columbia
Institute of Technology Aerospace Program, where hundreds of students learn how to
repair and fly the planes in the sky above (3800 Cessna Drive, Richmond, BC V7B 1C3).

58_ The Last Game Ball

The rise and fall of the Mighty Grizz

Just like the now-defunct NBA Vancouver Grizzlies, this particular relic is an underappreciated, misunderstood, and almost-lost gem, tucked away in the BC Sports Hall of Fame, an impressive, 15,000-square-foot facility chronicling all important things, people, and teams related to pro and amateur sports in the province through 27,000 artefacts. This story is about just one of them: a single, lonely basketball.

It is hard to believe that the same city that enthusiastically supported an NBA sports franchise from 1995 to 2001 has a hall of fame that only holds one measly basketball today. It's the game ball used during the last match of the Grizzlies' first season, and it's signed by some of the players and coaches. Sadly, just like the Mighty Grizz, perennial cellar dwellers in the league, the basketball is on the bottom row of a glass display case.

The rest of the museum has a large number of great highlights, including galleries devoted to the Vancouver Canucks and the BC Lions, plus several exciting exhibits dedicated to Canadian Heroes Terry Fox and Rick Hansen. One of the best parts of the hall of fame is the tribute to local Formula One racing driver Greg Moore. They have his actual car parked in the hall, plus walls and walls of racing paraphernalia. Don't miss the large, historical 2010 Olympic Winter Games display and some of the interactive attractions.

But why don't the Grizzlies rate a bigger display? Is it because they were unpopular? No, they were loved by all and provided fantastic entertainment, athleticism, and excitement on the hardwood for years. They used to pack GM Place. The problem was that during the six seasons they played in Vancouver, players' salaries doubled, while the Canadian dollar plummeted from 90 to 64 cents US. So, almost like TV's beloved *Beverly Hillbillies,* they "loaded up the truck, and they moved to Tennessee."

Address Gate A, BC Place, 777 Pacific Boulevard, Vancouver, BC V6B 4Y8, +1 (604) 687-5520, www.bcsportshall.com | Getting there SkyTrain to Stadium-Chinatown (Expo Line); ferry to Plaza of Nations dock | Hours Wed–Sun 10am–5pm | Tip Not far from the Hall of Fame, the Downtown Robert Lee YMCA, with a 1941 brick façade and plenty of open gym time for pick-up games, is worth a visit (995 Burrard Street, Vancouver, BC V6Z 1Y2).

59 Leg-In-Boot Square

Where gruesome mementos wash up

It is quite something to watch the constant flow of walkers, runners, and bike peddlers making their way past Leg-In-Boot Square, oblivious to the disturbing origins of its name. To be fair, the square is easy to overlook and doesn't seem in the least bit ominous. In fact, the view from the square looking north toward the boardwalk, the marina, and beyond the water toward the modern architecture of Yaletown is really quite pleasing. But it's a far cry from that strange day in 1887, when local constables found a dismembered leg, still wearing a boot, washed up on the beach near this spot.

Today, a crack team of forensic experts would have been dispatched to the scene, DNA samples taken, and databases consulted. But back then, the local constables had no idea what to do with the boot or the body part. They certainly didn't want it in the unrefrigerated precinct office. So they hung it outside, hoping, perhaps, that its owner might hop by and claim it. But they waited in vain. Nobody wanted the lonely leg, and the owner of the leg in the boot remains a mystery to this day.

One may imagine this sort of thing happens only once in a rare while, but it happens more often than you might think. Over a dozen feet have washed up on British Columbia's beaches in the past 10 years. In each case, only one foot has been found, and always still wearing a shoe.

The human mind immediately suspects foul play, but rational minds who know about these things explain that while bodies decomposing in water are apt to fall apart at the neck, wrists, and ankles, it's the running shoes that keep the feet preserved and help them float around in the ocean currents. Still, you have to wonder what happened to the original owner of the leg that washed up here. If there's a place somewhere around the world called 'Missing A Leg Square', the mystery could be solved.

Address Leg-In-Boot Square, Vancouver, BC V5Z 4B5 | Getting there By car, two-hour street parking is available on Moberly Road; water taxi to Stamp's Landing Ferry Dock | Hours Unrestricted | Tip Branas Mediterranean Grill is a short walk away and a great place to relax by the shore (617 Stamps Landing, Vancouver, BC V5Z 3Z1, www.branasgrill.ca).

60__Liberty Bakery + Cafe
Authentic Main Street culture

Main Street has many attractions, and Liberty Bakery + Cafe is one of them. It started thirty years ago as a retirement project for Swedish baker Gunnar Gustafson and his wife Liberty. There have been new owners since then, but the name remains the same, and the baked goods coming out of the ovens still hold the warmth and charm of Gunnar's Nordic sensibilities.

The building, circa 1912, is typical of the sort found on Main Street – unassuming, well-worn, and cosy. The hardwood floors are as full of character as the vintage oil paintings on the walls, a collection of portraits that might fool you into thinking you are resting at a café in Europe or some hidden mews frequented by artists and intellectuals.

In addition to a variety of caffeinated drinks created by skilled baristas, you'll enjoy butter croissants freshly baked on site, kouign amann, scones, biscuits, muffins, and cookies, plus delicious soup and sandwich options. The black bean soup has been on the menu for decades and is a neighbourhood favourite. The croque monsieur is *delicieux*. If you love a well-made sourdough loaf, you'll want to take advantage of the popular Bread Club created precisely for those who share this passion. You can pick up a loaf of crunchy-on-the-outside, soft-on-the-inside, bread any day, or you can subscribe to get a loaf every week. Each loaf is made on site in the Liberty kitchen.

In addition to being a classic staple of authentic Main Street culture, Liberty is your perfect jumping-off point for a Main Street shopping expedition. To the South, for reasons unknown, the shop names get more interesting. The Tooth Booth will check your teeth, and Eyepod Eyecare will check your eyes. To the North and all around are shops selling vintage clothing, antique furniture, musical instruments, contemporary fashion, books, and everything in between. Each shop is a one-of-a-kind gem.

Address 3699 Main Street, Vancouver, BC V5V 3N6, +1 (604) 709-9999, www.liberty-bakery.com | Getting there By car, parking is available at Lot 105 (3333 Main Street | Hours Daily 9am–4pm | Tip The Soap Dispensary just across the street is Vancouver's "first dedicated refill shop," selling soaps and other cleaning and beauty products (3718 Main Street, Vancouver, BC V5V 3N7, www.thesoapdispensary.com).

61 Lions Gate Bridge Lights
Gracie's Necklace

Vancouver's equivalent to San Francisco's Golden Gate Bridge is the Lions Gate Bridge. Rich in folklore and history, the bridge was completed in 1939 and entirely funded by the Irish Guinness family (of beer fame). The three-lane suspension bridge cost $6 million to build. The family primarily invested in the crossing because they had purchased 4,000 acres of land on the North Shore for $18.75 an acre in 1932, and the new bridge connected that vast wilderness to the young city of Vancouver, thus expediting development and increasing their land's value. In 1962, the Guinness family sold the bridge to the province of BC. But their involvement didn't end there, thanks to a World's Fair, a savvy local politician, and her penchant for large, flashy necklaces.

In 1986, the World's Fair took place in Vancouver with a number of beautification and restoration projects leading up to it. The high-ranking provincial minister responsible for bringing the fair to BC was Grace McCarthy. She recognised that if the province was inviting the world to the city, then its iconic bridge needed to shine. The suspension bridge had inadequate lighting and was barely visible at night. McCarthy orchestrated a donation from the Guinness family to fund strings of lights that were added to its cables and revealed the bridge's charms and splendid glory to the 22 million visitors who came to Vancouver. The lights, dubbed Gracie's Necklace, were turned on for the first time on February 19, 1986 and have been shining every night since then.

To prepare for the next big event that Vancouver hosted, the 2010 Olympic Winter Games, and to reduce energy costs, the original lights were replaced in July 2009 with 100-watt mercury vapour bulbs.

Grace McCarthy passed away in 2017 at the age of 89. Raise a pint of Guinness to Amazing Grace, whose legacy lives on in the bridge's evening glow.

Address Between the Stanley Park Causeway in Vancouver to Marine Drive in North Vancouver, www.th.gov.bc.ca/ATIS/lgcws/index.html | Getting there By car, closest public parking is available at Prospect Point | Hours Unrestricted | Tip On the Stanley Park side of the Lions Gate Bridge sit two majestic lions guarding the entrance to the bridge. These imposing cast-concrete beasts were the work of sculptor Charles Marega. People sometimes dress them up in outfits on special occasions and holidays.

62 The Living Roof

An unconventional roof on the Convention Centre

Vancouver's quest to become the greenest city in the world is nowhere more evident than from the roof of its billion-dollar Convention Centre. The six-acre living roof that sits atop the massive waterfront structure is the largest of its kind in Canada. It features over 400,000 plants native to British Columbia, which provide insulation against the cold of winter and the heat of summer. The roof is the most prominent example of the building's long-term commitment to the environment, and it is also the largest non-industrial living roof in North America.

Other eco-friendly features of the building include a seawater heating and cooling system, and an on-site water treatment plant. A special fish habitat was incorporated into the building's ocean foundation so as not to disturb an historic salmon migration path, and four buzzing colonies of bees live on the roof, supplying one of the centre's restaurants with honey. Ornamental BC lumber from sustainably managed forests is widely used throughout the facility's tasteful interior.

The Convention Centre has won countless sustainability awards. It was used as the International Broadcast Centre for the 2010 Olympic Winter Games, and it now hosts over 500 events a year. Despite the building's busy schedule, the operators still find time to mow and water the roof. Of course the building's wastewater is treated and reused for the roof's irrigation.

Just below, you'll find the main 53,000-square-foot ballroom with stunning views of the harbour and the mountains. If you think mowing the roof is a big job, just be glad you don't have to clean the 55-foot-high windows in that ballroom. The centre only uses Green Seal and EcoLogo cleaning products and was the world's first Double LEED Platinum convention centre. And it goes without saying – smoking is most definitely not allowed on the premises.

Address Vancouver Convention Centre, West Building, 1055 Canada Place, Vancouver, BC V6C 0C3, www.vancouverconventioncentre.com | Getting there By car, metered parking is available nearby, and underground paid parking available in the Convention Centre | Hours See website for tour information | Tip It rains a lot in Vancouver, as the 65-foot blue raindrop sculpture on the waterfront side of the Convention Centre reminds us. The work was installed in 2009 by a group of German artists known collectively as Inges Idee.

63 Long Table Distillery
Vancouver's first micro-distillery

Long Table Distillery was originally inspired by British Columbia's wild West Coast wilderness. Since it opened in 2010, its small staff of three or four people has been passionately devoted to the fine art of copper-pot distilling small batch spirits, to the great delight of loyal customers and fans of their gins, vodkas, and other such treats.

You'll find his unique micro-distillery nestled under the shadow of the Granville Street Bridge in a hip, old, light-industrial area that is quickly sprouting high-rise condos. As you enter, you'll immediately be struck by the tasting room's eponymous centrepiece, a 14-foot-long table carved out of a giant British Columbia Sequoia tree. Behind the table is the heart of the operation: a 300-gallon copper pot full of interesting valves, pipes, round windows, and spigots. Charles will be more than happy to explain how it works while pointing out the importance of the local ingredients that go into each handmade batch. The botanicals are hand-picked by a network of expert wildlife foragers from the local mountains.

A secret this good is hard to keep quiet. The cache that British Columbia's rugged coastline, pristine waterways, and alpine meadows possess have proven to be quite the draw for international spirit connoisseurs. Since opening, the small shop has begun to export their spirits worldwide to cities including London.

From Friday to Sunday they open up the 50-seat tasting lounge for cocktail service. There's also a limited snack menu of charcuterie, olives and nuts. Long Table Distillery also features a retail sales section where customers can purchase any of their small-batch, premium quality gins and seasonal spirits, as well as a variety of bar tools, like strainers, juicers, shakers, and tumblers, along with garnishes, bitters, tonics, elixirs, and mixers.

If you are into something a little adventurous while you are there, try the Cucumber Gin.

Address 1428 Granville Street, Vancouver, BC V6Z 1N2, +1 (604) 266-0177, www.longtabledistillery.com, info@longtabledistillery.com | Getting there By car, Advanced Parking at 1380 Burrard Street | Hours See website for visiting hours | Tip Look for Vancouver House, the newest and most unusual apartment building in the city, a block away. It's the fourth-tallest building in the city, and some say it looks like a Lego project in progress (1480 Howe Street, Vancouver, BC V6Z 1C4, www.vancouverhouse.ca).

64 Lord Byng High School
Archie and Veronica's Alma Mater

It looks like the quintessential American high school, a fortified, three-story, red-brick building constructed in the 1920s. It is the wholesome cornerstone of a quiet, tree-lined neighbourhood and built to last for centuries. A solid, respected pillar of academia. Its neoclassical architecture oozes small-town USA. The only problem is that it is not located in any of the 50 states.

For the viewers of the long list of TV shows and movies shot at Lord Byng High School, it doesn't really matter. Perception is reality and this school does a great job of faking it. Vancouver, sometimes referred to as Hollywood North, has a robust movie industry partly because of its spectacular scenery, partly because of the low Canadian dollar, partly because of its huge talent base, and partly because of great set locations like Lord Byng.

A partial list of TV shows and movies that were shot at Lord Byng includes *The X-Files*, *X-Men Origins*, *Pretty Little Liars*, *Swindle*, *Saving Silverman*, *The Boy Who Could Fly*, *Mr. Young*, *Emily Owens M.D.*, *Masters of Horror*, *Hollow Man 2*, and, of course, *Riverdale*, where it doubles as Archie's school.

The high school takes up an entire city block at 16th and Crown and was named after Field Marshall Julian Hedworth George Byng, who fought in World War I and went on to become the 12th Governor General of Canada. Today, having movies and TV shows shot on location is probably a good thing for the student body. The school is renowned for its arts programs, particularly media arts.

In real life the school boasts some notable alumni. Popular Canadian folk/indie musician Dan Mangan, who has won two Juno Awards, went to Lord Byng, along with Ross Rebagliati, the first person ever to win a gold medal in snowboarding at the Winter Olympic Games. One of the stars from the CBS Sitcom *How I Met Your Mother*, Cobie Smulders, also graduated from Lord Byng.

Address 3939 West 16th Avenue, Vancouver, BC V6R 3L9, +1 (604) 713-8171, byng.vsb.bc.ca | Getting there By car, street parking is available nearby | Hours Unrestricted from the outside only | Tip Cheapskates, Vancouver's oldest and best-known second-hand sports store, is just down the street from the school (3644 West 16th Avenue, Vancouver, BC V6R 3C4, www.cheapskatesvancouver.com).

65 Lulu Line Ghost Rails

Clickity-clack, will they ever come back?

No, they probably won't ever come back. But for the time being, you can still see some of the few remains of the tracks that once connected Vancouver with Steveston over a century ago. One of the best places to see them is at the bucolic intersection of First and Fir Streets. Partially hidden by foliage and lost in the no man's land between parking lots and condos, the railroad tracks laid out before you are remnants of the Lulu Line. The Lulu Line was initially created by the Vancouver and Lulu Island Railway in 1901, then purchased by the Canadian Pacific Railway (CPR) in 1902 and leased to the BC Electric Railway Company (BCER) in 1905, long before rails were replaced by rubber in the 1950s.

Starting from this First and Fir location, you can walk along the abandoned tracks for about a block before the rails run out and the track fades into a gravel bed separating two parking lots at Fir Street and Second Avenue. Gaze south across Second Avenue and you'll notice an extraordinarily large alley between the two buildings there. That's where the tracks used to keep running on down toward Fir and Fifth, and where the Arbutus Greenway bike path and running trail now takes over. Check this area out on the satellite view of Google maps and you can clearly trace the tracks' easterly trail through the brush toward Burrard Street where they used to connect with the City and Suburban tram lines running from Kitsilano to downtown via the old Granville trestle bridge at that location.

We like to think that everything in the past was slow and in-efficient, but these rails were capable of transporting people from Vancouver to Steveston in just about as much time as it would take by public transportation today. Given contemporary concerns about burning fossil fuels, it makes one wonder if they should have kept the Lulu Line rolling after all.

Address Intersection of First and Fir Streets, Vancouver, BC V6J 1G1 | Getting there
By car, closest paid parking is the Impark lot at 1585 West 2nd Avenue; by ferry, closest
dock is Granville Island dock | Hours Unrestricted | Tip Only seven of the original
BC Electric Railway tram cars survive, and you can see a beautifully preserved one at the
Steveston Interurban Tram Building (4011 Moncton Street, Richmond, BC V7E 3A8,
www.richmond.ca/culture/sites/tram/abouttram.htm).

66 The Marine Building

The most interesting building in Vancouver

When Vancouver Mayor Malkin launched construction of The Marine Building in 1929 with a hearty blow on a golden whistle, many local people had never heard about skyscrapers and few would have ever seen one. Even the building's architects had only created one previously. Nonetheless, it became one of the finest examples of art deco architecture in the world.

Drawing upon the city's maritime history and natural environment for inspiration, it was designed to resemble "some great crag rising from the sea, clinging with sea flora and fauna, tinted in sea-green, touched with gold." When its 21 floors reaching 97 metres into the sky were completed the following year, it was the tallest building in the city, and briefly, the tallest building in the British Empire. It would remain the tallest building in Vancouver until 1967. And at a cost of $2.3 million, it was also outrageously expensive. The first owner, reeling from the price tag and cash-strapped by the Great Depression, sold it before the paint was dry.

Walk around the exterior of the Marine Building and examine the exquisite terracotta panels, gaze in awe at its impressive brass doors, peek within its stately and impressive foyer, and discover the stylised depictions of the technologies and human enterprises that were rapidly changing the world at that time, including biplanes, steam trains, steam ships, and a zeppelin. Starfish, shells, fish, and seahorses comprise some of the numerous marine themes built into its design. And don't miss the whimsical foyer clock with fish and crabs in place of numbers.

While its cost, height, and super-fast elevators made it famous back in the 1930s, its style is what keeps it famous today. You might even recognise it as The Daily Planet building in the television show *Smallville* or as the comic book superhero lair The Baxter Building in the *Fantastic Four* movies.

Address 355 Burrard Street, Vancouver, BC V6C 0B2 | Getting there By car, closest paid parking is the Metro Parking lot no. 66 located at 401 Burrard Street | Hours Mon – Fri 8:30am – 5pm | Tip Two kilometres south on Burrard Street you'll find another of Vancouver's art deco wonders in the Burrard Bridge (Burrard Street, Vancouver, BC V5K 0A1, www.vancouverhistory.ca/archives_burrard.htm). Clever observers will note that portraits of Captain George Vancouver and Sir Harry Burrard flank the piers. The braziers at either end honour those who served in World War I.

67 __ Monstrous Sturgeon Fish

Back from the brink at the Vancouver Aquarium

They are massive, they are prehistoric looking, and these sturgeon call Vancouver home. Well, at least the Fraser River. If you ever catch one, don't even bother telling your friends unless you have a picture because they are so big that no one will believe you. The largest white sturgeon ever caught on the Fraser weighed a whopping 1,800 pounds and was 18 feet long. Four- to six-footers are common, and these fish can live up to 200 years.

The average Vancouverite hardly knows that these whoppers even exist. Furthermore, they are unaware that they are swimming below them when they cross the Oak Street and Knight Street bridges and swimming above them when they commute through the Massey Tunnel. They're everywhere though, sucking up prey through their ventral vacuum-like mouths and simply enjoying being big fish.

Sturgeon are a relative of the dinosaur, and their appearance has remained unchanged for over 175 million years. Nonetheless, they are not that well known in the city, perhaps because 50 years ago, they almost became extinct. Their roe was coveted as luxury caviar, and their meat was sold around the world. Thus, overfishing resulted in dangerously low levels of this amazing, elongated creature. But thanks to the efforts of the Fraser River Sturgeon Conservation Society and a catch and release program they introduced, sturgeon are once again calling the muddy Fraser River home. They are at the top of the food chain there, and humans are their only predators.

The best place for a selfie with a sturgeon is in the Vancouver Aquarium. But they're not that easy to find among the 300 other species of fish in this world-class facility. On the main floor, look for a display called 'Treasures of the BC Coast', where you'll find several medium-sized sturgeon. Two more of these monsters live downstairs in the 'Pacific Canada Strait of Georgia' tank.

Address 845 Avison Way, Vancouver, BC V6G 3E2, +1 (604) 659-3474, www.vanaqua.org, visitorexperience@ocean.org | Getting there By car, parking is available at the aquarium | Hours Daily 10am–5pm | Tip Walk northeast to the seawall and see Elek Imredy's sculpture, *Girl in a Wetsuit*. Created in 1972, it is now one of Vancouver's iconic artworks (2743 Stanley Park Drive, Vancouver, BC V6G 3E2).

68 Museum of Anthropology

Once a fort for defence, now a font of knowledge

Best known for its collection of Northwest Coast First Nations' art, the Museum of Anthropology (MOA) is a sensorial treasure trove of local and international cultural artefacts not to be missed. As soon as you arrive, the towering totem poles and mythical creatures carved from wood let you know you're in the right place.

But before you rush inside, stand back and take a moment to consider the building itself. It may be over 40 years old, but the design by famed Canadian architect Arthur Erickson retains a contemporary, modern look even though it is inspired by traditional Northwest Coast First Nations' post-and-beam structures. Tucked in among natural coastal foliage, towering cedar trees, and a calming coastal water feature, the building echoes and reflects the past, as do the objects on display inside.

A fascinating and less well-known quirk of the design is that it is built upon the old military installation that once stood here. Looking around the peaceful and serene site, it's hard to believe it was once the most heavily armed of five coast artillery forts built in 1939 to defend the port of Vancouver during World War II. In fact, its long-gone three guns had enough power to send a projectile clear across English Bay.

Once you go inside the museum, you'll find the concrete remains of Gun Number 2 is now home to Bill Reid's iconic *Raven and the First Men* sculpture. This impressive sculpture, which took two years to make, is carved from a four-and-a-half-ton block of laminated yellow cedar and depicts the origins of man according to Haida legend. Prince Charles formally unveiled the work in 1980, but many Canadians saw it for the first time in 2004, printed on the 20-dollar bill. There are some 50,000 ethnographic objects in the museum from Asia, the Americas, South Pacific, Africa, and Europe, making this a place you'll probably have to visit more than once.

Address 6393 Northwest Marine Drive, Vancouver, BC V6T 1Z2, +1 (604) 822-5087, www.moa.ubc.ca, info@moa.ubc.ca | Getting there By car, paid parking is available at the museum lot | Hours Check website for hours | Tip Koerner's Pub is just around the corner from the museum and a favourite watering hole for anthropologists and other academics (6371 Crescent Road, Vancouver, BC V6T 1Z2, www.koerners.ca).

69 Mushroom Studios
Little ship full of dreams

What is a recording studio if not a ship full of dreams? Did the five members of Heart ever dream in 1975 that their Vancouver recordings of hits like "Dreamboat Annie", "Crazy On You", and "Magic Man" would make them famous? When they recorded their debut album here, did they dare to dream that one day they'd be inducted into the Rock and Roll Hall of Fame? It's impossible to say. But surely many dreams – and perhaps some heartbreak – are associated with this nondescript birthplace of several touchstones of the rock world.

Soon after opening in 1966, the studio attracted a number of talented artists. Diana Ross and The Supremes were among the first to use the facility. The dynamic damsels from Detroit were in town for a week-long gig at The Cave Club and needed to record something to go along with their recent guest appearances on the hit 1960s' TV show *Tarzan*. Robert Plant was also among the earliest to visit Mushroom in the late 1960s, laying down some harmonica tracks for "Bring It On Home". The studio picked up momentum in the 1970s with Terry Jacks' 1973 recording "Seasons in the Sun". That same year, Mushroom was the birthplace of the Incredible Bongo Band's cover of "Apache" – a track so influential in hip-hop that it inspired the documentary *Sample This*. Iconic Canadian artists like Bachman Turner Overdrive followed by taking care of business here, Trooper raised a little hell here, and Loverboy decided this was a place where they could be turned loose. Later on, Vancouver's 54-40, Carly Rae Jepsen, Sarah McLachlan, and Spirit of the West all passed through here on the way to fame and fortune.

Over its colourful life, Mushroom Studios has had a few different names and owners. Today, it is home to Afterlife Studios, a place where artists can still record 'old-school' on analogue recording equipment. But whatever you call it, the building is still a ship full of dreams.

Address 1234 West 6th Avenue, Vancouver, BC V6H 1A5, www.afterlifestudiosvancouver.com/history | **Getting there** By car, street parking is available on Alder Street | **Hours** Unrestricted from the outside only | **Tip** If music and history are two of your passions, check out The Warehouse, the recording studio created by Bryan Adams in a restored 1886 Gastown warehouse (100 Powell Street, Vancouver, BC V6A 1G1, www.warehousestudio.com).

70__The Naam

Peace, love, and vegetables

During the Summer of Love in 1967 and the psychedelic years that ensued, the groovy strip along West 4th Avenue in Vancouver was a famous hippie hangout where tourists came from across Canada to spot and photograph those crazy longhairs. 4th Avenue was known as 'Rainbow Road', and its epicentre was a small restaurant and natural food store.

The counterculture movement that was born in the mid-1960s at the intersection of Haight and Ashbury in San Francisco spread to 4th and McDonald in Vancouver. Only a handful of the storefronts from that era are still in business today, and the famous Naam restaurant is one of them. It was established in 1968, which allows it to lay claim as Vancouver's oldest natural food restaurant. At one time, it was managed by a loose, idealistic co-op of its workers. The bohemian vibe from over 50 years ago, overflowing with peace and love and music, is still alive at The Naam. The restaurant's name has nothing to do with the war-torn Asian country that fuelled many of the protests at the time. That said, many sit-ins or demonstrations may well have been planned there since it was a hub for anti-war activists and environmentalists, including the early members of Greenpeace. *Naam* is a Sanskrit word that means 'name', as in 'the name of God'.

The Naam still specialises in delicious vegetarian and vegan dishes – try the amazing Dragon Rice Bowl – and still has an atmosphere right out of a Grateful Dead poster. The food is healthy and plentiful, the place often has a long line, and on most evenings, they continue to have live music. The restaurant also has a nice outdoor patio in the summer time and a cozy fireplace in the winter. For all the early-rising hippies out there, the Naam serves a delicious breakfast from 6am to 11:30am. As with all restaurants today, it's non-smoking, so you may choose to toke on that reefer before entering.

Address 2724 West 4th Avenue, Vancouver, BC 6K 1R1, +1 (604) 738-7151,
www.thenaam.com, info@thenaam.com | Getting there By car, metered parking is available
on 4th Avenue | Hours Mon–Thu 8am–midnight, Fri & Sat 8am–3am, Sun 9am–mid-
night | Tip Canada recently legalised the use of marijuana, and the first pot shop in
Vancouver to be legally licensed by the Provincial Government to sell recreational weed, the
Evergreen Cannabis Society, is just down the street (2868 West 4th Avenue, Vancouver,
BC V6K 1R2, www.evergreencannabissociety.com).

71 Nat Bailey Stadium

The last unexceptional sports stadium in Vancouver

One of the great charms of the Nat Bailey Stadium is that there's nothing exceptional about it at all. In these high-tech days, where every sports arena is renowned for its gargantuan dimensions, huge audience capacity, mega-signage, and comfortable seating, the Nat stands out as perhaps one of the last authentic sports stadiums of days gone by. Grab a beer, eat a hotdog, and watch a baseball game just like they did when the place was built in 1951.

In addition to its merits as a piece of no-nonsense sports infrastructure, the Nat is a piece of living sports history. One of Minor League Baseball's most historic sites, it was initially built to host the Vancouver Capilanos and was originally called the Capilano Stadium. But as the Capilanos were replaced by the Oakland Oaks, and the Oaks replaced by the Vancouver Mounties, and the Mounties replaced by the Vancouver Canadians, the name of the stadium became less and less meaningful. This created an opportunity to rename the place and, in 1978, it was named after one of Vancouver's biggest baseball fans, Mr Nathaniel 'Nat' Bailey.

Though baseball was his passion, Mr Nat Bailey is probably better appreciated by Vancouverites as the owner and originator of the White Spot restaurant franchise. The connection between baseball and fast food is inseparable and started in the 1920s, when the young, American-born entrepreneur sold peanuts, hot dogs, and ice cream from his converted 1918 Model T truck to crowds at local baseball games.

The Nat has a little-known connection with Seattle baseball history. Some of the stadium is made from recycled parts of Seattle's Sick's Stadium, which was built in 1939 and named after Emil Sick, owner of the Rainier Brewing Company. When that stadium was demolished in 1979, Vancouver Canadians' owner Harry Ornest bought $60,000-worth of its remnants and had it all shipped north.

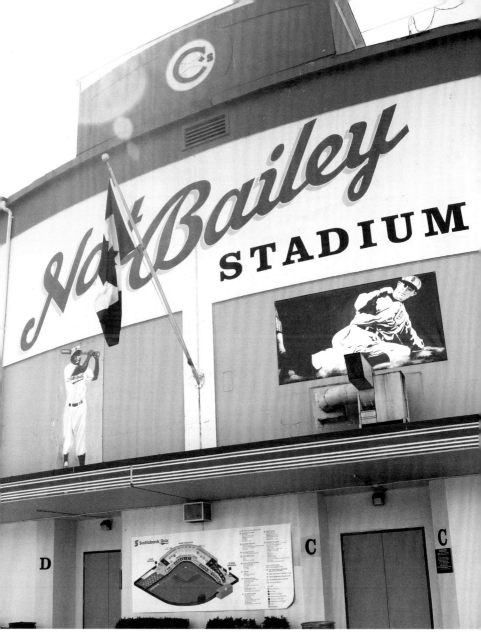

Address 4601 Ontario Street, Vancouver, BC V5V 3H4, www.milb.com | Getting there By bicycle, via the Ontario Street Greenway; by car, paid parking is available at the park on game days | Hours See website for seasonal hours and event schedule | Tip The Vancouver 2010 Olympic and Paralympic Winter Games' curling venue and current home to the Vancouver Curling Club is a short stroll away (4575 Clancy Loranger Way, Vancouver, BC V5Y 2M4, www.vancurl.com).

72 The Nemesis Building
Grab a cuppa inside a work of art

An art school in the trendy, gentrified part of town is bound to be oozing with creative energy. The new Emily Carr University of Art + Design is no exception. For its students, one of the epicentres of innovation and original, imaginative ideas is Nemesis, the on-campus coffee shop. This place is unlike anywhere you have ever been before and is itself an architectural example of creative genius.

The fabulous, curvy exterior of Nemesis is a striking, giant, bulb shape with onion-like overlapping leaves surrounding it. Painted the shiniest, brightest red colour ever, it boldly jumps out at anyone driving by on the Great Northern Way. But do stop and admire the outside, and then go inside to enjoy another masterpiece of design. In the centre of the round, 186-square-metre (2,000-square-foot) building is a big skylight that you can't miss because the ribbed cloth drapes fan out from it in an intricate, 360-degree pattern. The drapes are a muted white colour that adds to the laid-back atmosphere inside. It's all very tastefully done – it's not your neighbourhood Starbucks.

Nemesis serves great coffee too. Whether made with the sleek, silver espresso machines, prepared at the pour-over bar, or simply brewed the plain, old-fashioned drip way, it's all good. The beans have been ethically sourced directly from trusted farmers. And speaking of sustainability, the building is certified LEED Gold. If you find that you have worked up a bit of an appetite while exploring Nemesis inside and out, you are at the right place, as fresh and locally sourced ingredients and an ever-rotating menu are the order of the day.

Vancouver has its fair share of amazingly interesting buildings. Most of them are houses, office towers, or museums. Nemesis is one of the most unique buildings and coffee shops in the world and a must-see for anyone who loves architecture and a rich cup of joe.

Address 555 Great Northern Way, Vancouver, BC V5T 1E1, www.nemesis.coffee |
Getting there By car, parking is available at Lot 017 (701 Great Northern Way) |
Hours Mon–Fri 8am–4pm, Sat & Sun 9am–5pm | Tip The Michael O'Brian
Exhibition Commons, next to the entrance lobby of the Emily Carr University of Art +
Design, hosts an ever changing exhibition of students' art, and entry is free (520 East
1st Avenue, Vancouver, BC V5T 1E1, www.ecuad.ca).

73__Neptoon Records
Tune in to vinyl

People of a certain age may remember the glory days of the vinyl record when recorded music was played on a blob of plastic that had been mechanically smooshed into a flat disc and impressed with a swirl of grooves that translated vibrations to melodies with the aid of a diamond-tipped needle dragged around it at different speeds. These records also came in attractive cardboard sleeves – album covers – that on occasion were as iconic as the sounds contained within. Who can forget the zipper on the classic Rolling Stones' *Sticky Fingers* album, the mesmerising prism on Pink Floyd's *Dark Side of the Moon*, or the low-hanging balls on Fleetwood Mac's *Rumours*?

If any of that rings a nostalgic bell, or perhaps whets your appetite to learn more, you need to explore Neptoon Records. It is not only Vancouver's oldest independent record store, but is also still managed by the same owner. Rob Frith first opened the doors of Neptoon Records in 1981, and since then, vinyl records have gone in and out of style several times. Now joined by son Ben, the shop is a destination for audiophiles of all types and, while they do have compact discs, it's the vinyl records that are the main attraction. Boxes and boxes of records are displayed just like they used to be back when it was normal for everyone to flip through stacks of them. Neptoon not only boasts the largest selection of used and new vinyl in the city, but also has their own label and makes their own records.

Keep your eyes peeled and you may even spot a music celebrity during your visit. Bo Diddley, Feist, Seth Rogen, Tom Waits, Marc Maron, and even local media personality Nardwuar the Human Serviette have all been to Neptoon. Visit soon or, better yet, attend one of the live performances that bands sometimes put on in the store. Word is that it can turn into the best party you've been to since college.

Address 3561 Main Street, Vancouver, BC V5V 3N4, +1 (604) 324-1229, www.neptoon.com | Getting there By car, metered parking is available on Main Street | Hours Mon–Sat 11am–6:30pm, Sun noon–5pm | Tip If you need vintage furniture to match your old-school record collection, check out ReFind Home Furnishings (4609 Main Street, Vancouver, BC V5V 3R6, www.refindhomefurnishings.com).

74_Nine O'Clock Gun

A blast from the past

All you have to do is listen: at exactly 9pm, if you are anywhere near the downtown core, you'll hear it. Every night for over 100 years, a 1,500-pound cast iron cannon sitting on the banks of the Stanley Park Seawall has discharged an empty artillery round creating a resounding deep booming blast so loud that even the seagulls on the Lions Gate Bridge flinch.

Vancouverites often mistake the jarring sound for a nearby car backfiring or for kids igniting firecrackers. But the gunfire actually originates from a muzzle-loaded cannon that was built in Woolwich, England in 1807.

In 1898, the gun was installed by the Canadian Department of Marine and Fisheries in the same spot where you will find it today. Overlooking Coal Harbour, it was originally intended to signal local fisherman that it was time to stop work and pull in their nets. At the turn of the last century, ships leaving the harbour relied on the sound to accurately set their chronometers, and nearby residents of a young Vancouver readjusted the hands on the stately grandfather clocks in their parlours to nine when they heard the cannon blast.

One day in the 1960s, pranksters tossed rocks into the cannon's muzzle, hurling them across the harbour later that evening. A commercial Esso Marine Gas Barge that used to float 400 yards offshore became a casualty when the discharged rocks blasted out the 'O' on the barge's huge illuminated red and blue ESSO sign. Bullseye! In that same crazy decade of pranks, some UBC engineering students stole the Nine O'Clock Gun and held it for ransom until a donation was made to BC Children's Hospital.

Today, the Nine O'Clock Gun sits behind a protective wire cage to deter any future hijinks. To prevent startling and shocking people taking their evening strolls on the Seawall, a flashing red light has been installed that warns of the imminent blast.

Address 1981 Stanley Park Drive, Vancouver, BC V6G 3E2 | Getting there By car, paid parking available near the totem poles | Hours Unrestricted | Tip There is a clock in Vancouver more famous than the Nine O'Clock Gun. It's the antique Steam Clock in Gastown, and it's not far from Stanley Park (305 Water Street, Vancouver, BC V6B 1B9). Why not go there at 9pm and listen for the blast to see if the two old-fashioned time pieces are in sync?

75 __Nitobe Memorial Garden
Serenity now

You might think of it simply as a tranquil Japanese garden – and you would be right – but the amount of symbolism and meaning packed into these 2.5 acres of beautiful UBC campus will astound the scholar and thrill the Japanophile. Named after renowned scholar and international statesman Inazo Nitobe (1862–1933), this authentic Japanese garden is a bio-tribute to his vision of a harmonious world.

As he created not only for aesthetic pleasure but also intellectual stimulation, designer Konosuke Mori of Chiba University filled the gardens with symbolism. For instance, the main path symbolises the eternal cycle of life and each of the six water crossings in the garden has its own significance as well. The 77-log bridge is symbolic of Nitobe's desire to be "a bridge over the Pacific," while a clever zigzag bridge by the iris pond is said to confound the devil because evil spirits travel in straight lines.

The island of eternity, with rocks strategically placed to give it the shape of a turtle, represents longevity. No man is an island, but it has been said that the flat-topped rock on the island, known as the *rahai seki*, represents Nitobe's soul.

If people were flowers, Inazo Nitobe was no shrinking violet. One of the earliest international students, he left Tokyo Imperial University in 1884 to study economics and political science at Johns Hopkins University in the US before getting his PhD at Halle University in Germany. Soon after, he had four more doctorates, a Western wife, became a Quaker, and was involved in the creation of the League of Nations. He told everyone to give peace a chance, decades before Yoko Ono turned the idea into a song.

As a much admired man in Japan, Nitobe was on the 5,000-yen currency note from 1984 to 2007. It will only cost a fraction of that to enter the gardens, a very affordable way to achieve peace of mind.

Address 1895 Lower Mall, Vancouver, BC V6T 1Z4, +1 (604) 822-6038, https://botanicalgarden.ubc.ca | Getting there By car, closest paid parking is UBC's Fraser River parking lot at 6440 Memorial Road | Hours See website for seasonal hours | Tip If the garden has stimulated your appetite for Japanese flavours, visit Hidekazu Tojo's restaurant for some of the best sushi this side of the Pacific (1133 West Broadway, Vancouver, BC V6H 1G1, www.tojos.com).

76 Old South Terminal Airport

A flight into the past

The Vancouver International Airport has been voted best airport in North America and best airport in the world several times by industry associations over the years. It's an efficient, modern operation servicing over 20 million passengers a year. But it wasn't always that way. In 1927, a man who was then and probably still is the world's most famous aviator, Charles Lindbergh, was asked to visit Vancouver after his celebrated non-stop solo Atlantic flight. His answer to the dignitaries who extended the friendly invitation was simply, "There is no fit field to land on." Two years after that curt refusal, city officials invested $600,000 into the future South Terminal, replacing the crude grass strip at Minoru Park that Lindbergh avoided. In 1932, the airport began scheduled services between Vancouver and Seattle. That year the airport serviced 1,070 passengers.

During World War II, the old South Terminal was leased to the Federal Government and operated by the Department of National Defence as a Royal Canadian Air Force Station. It was used as part of the British Commonwealth Air Training Plan, and the service men and women who were stationed there lived in a nearby 300-unit housing complex that still stands today, called Burkville. A fire destroyed the original terminal in 1949, and in 1950 a new one was built.

In 1968, the present main terminal was completed and the old South Terminal began to serve as a satellite operation for small charter flights flying to fishing camps and other out-of-the-way destinations. Of course the old terminal has a more laid-back, unhurried feel. Be sure to take your time while you are there to have a look at the wall covered in old black-and-white shots of Vancouver aviation history. The building also has a papier mâché floatplane and grey seagull hanging from the ceiling along with the occasional old propeller hanging on a wall.

Address 4440 Cowley Crescent, Richmond, BC V7B 1B8, +1 (604) 207-7077, www.yvr.ca/en/passengers/transportation/airport-south | Getting there SkyTrain to YVR-Airport (Canada Line), then take the courtesy shuttle from Bus Bay 3 on the second level of YVR International Arrivals to the old airport | Hours Daily 5:45am – 10:45pm | Tip An amazing place to watch floatplanes land and take off from the Fraser River is The Flying Beaver Bar and Grill, not far from the Old South Terminal (4760 Inglis Drive, Richmond, BC V7B 1W4, www.mjg.ca/flying-beaver).

77 __Original Fluevog Store
A platform for shoes

For fashion fiends and footwear fanciers, this shop is where the fascinating fantasy of Fluevog fame first found favour. From these humble roots grew one of Vancouver's most successful footwear brands. Today, John Fluevog is a celebrated Canadian business entrepreneur whose creations have been coveted and flaunted by movie stars, pop stars, and artists for nearly 50 years. Madonna, Beyoncé, Lady Gaga, Lady Miss Kier, Alice Cooper, and Jack White have all worn Fluevogs. But back in 1970, these achievements were just a dream to the flashy, flamboyant youngster who partnered with Peter Fox to create Fox and Fluevog.

The neighbourhood had not yet had its makeover. Verne Simpson's statue of Gassy Jack had not yet been installed on the site of the old Maple Tree, and Maple Tree Square was still being retrofitted with cobblestones to make it look suitably old-timey. But the timing was right, and from this location Fox and Fluevog catered to the fashion-forward footwear aficionados of the day, offering shoes inspired by bold, confident designs of the American cars of the 1950s and 1960s that John grew up around, and by funky turn-of-the-century footwear fashions John had previously discovered in Mexico. Soon, John and Peter were able to open another store on Granville Street, and by 1980, John was able to branch out on his own as John Fluevog Shoes. The rest, as they say, is history. From the disco era to the grunge era, in rock and pop, on the dance floor or the mosh pit, on the silver screen, and on the soles of many a Vancouverite walking the pavements of Gastown and the sidewalks of Granville Street and beyond, Fluevog shoes have been at the forefront of footed fashion. And it all began right here.

Today, number 2 Powell is home to Angel Vancouver, the city's first Desigual clothing boutique. Ask owner Jackie Haliburton about the poem Leonard Cohen is said to have written on the exterior wall.

Address 2 Powell Street, Vancouver, BC V6A 1E7, www.fluevog.com | Getting there
By car, closest paid parking is EasyPark Lot 31 at 160 Water Street, metered parking
is available nearby | Hours Viewable from the outside at any time | Tip Fluevog still
has a store in Gastown, just a block away (68 Water Street, Vancouver, BC V6B 1A4,
www.fluevog.com/stores/vancouver-gastown). In addition to being a retail shop, it is
also a design shop and headquarters for the Fluevog empire.

78_Ovaltine Café

Neon memories

When FBI Agent Fox Mulder needed a slice of lemon pie and a cup of coffee, where did he go? Why, the Ovaltine Café of course! Because the Ovaltine is a dead ringer for that place you always seem to see in cop shows and noir mysteries.

It achieves its 1940s' vibe honestly because hardly anything has changed at the Ovaltine since the doors opened in 1942. The booths, the tables, and the chairs are all pretty much as they were back in the day. In fact, authenticity is what the Ovaltine is all about. You'll find nothing fake or pretentious here, from the sign outside, to the furnishings inside, to the dishes cooked in the kitchen, to the customers eating out front. There's almost nothing on the menu that costs over $10, and you won't get a more honest burger, meatloaf, or mac and cheese anywhere else. The Ovaltine milkshake is made with real ice cream and real Ovaltine. Owner Grace Chen and her daughter Rachel make sure there's always a place for the working man or woman to get a hearty meal.

But one of the most remarkable things not to have changed since 1942 is the iconic neon sign outside the restaurant. The sign is one of the few remaining echoes of the days when Vancouver had more neon than anywhere else in the world except Shanghai, China. Vancouver's neon boom began in the 1940s and the Ovaltine sign was among Vancouver's first. The trend grew so quickly that by 1953, the Neon Products Company boasted that Vancouver had over 19,000 of the colourful beacons of commerce. That all changed in the 1970s, when City Hall decided peak neon had been achieved. With new signs discouraged, and with established businesses changing locations and names, the signs of yesterday began to slowly fade from sight. Except for the Ovaltine, where the neon shines as bright as the day it was first illuminated, and where the meatloaf still warms the heart as well as the stomach.

Address 251 East Hastings Street, Vancouver, BC V6A 1P2, +1 (604) 685-7021, www.ovaltinecafe.ca | Getting there By car, metered parking is available on East Hastings Street | Hours Daily 8am–3pm | Tip Many of the iconic original signs of yesteryear can be found at the Museum of Vancouver (1100 Chestnut Street, Vancouver, BC V6J 3J9, www.museumofvancouver.ca).

79 Point Grey Road Bike Path
Cycling success

Vancouver's bold initiative to become the greenest city in the world by 2020 is outlined in a 90-page action plan. In the thick document, the city commits to making cycling a practical way of getting around. The stated goal is for half the trips Vancouverites make to be on foot or by bike. In 2016, City Council put its money where its mouth is by spending over six million dollars to convert one of Vancouver's most prestigious car traffic arteries into a bike path.

The site of the car-free zone was Point Grey Road. The old ocean-side road is also known as the Golden Mile because some of the most expensive houses in Canada line it. Lululemon founder Chip Wilson has a shack on the waterfront side of the street that was assessed at over $75 million.

Before the conversion, Point Grey Road carried over 10,000 cars a day. Today, you don't have to worry about those cars anymore because they have gone on to congest other routes, like 4th Avenue and Broadway. But watch out for the cyclists. Up to 2,700 riders on your average weekday make it one of the busiest bike paths in a city that is becoming more bike-friendly each year.

Aside from moving four-wheel traffic congestion somewhere else, the bike path was controversial because of its width. Some felt it was too wide, but it's that very width that allows it to accommodate all sorts of vehicles. At 25 feet across, the path allows cyclists, skateboarders, rollerbladers, pedestrians, and dog walkers to coexist.

The Point Grey Road Bike Path is now part of the beautiful 17-mile Seaside Greenway that starts downtown at the Vancouver Convention Centre, winds around the Stanley Park Seawall, goes along the shore of English Bay and False Creek, and then ends at Spanish Banks. One warning: when you ride your bike through the Point Grey Road section, keep an eye out for the occasional Rolls-Royce backing out of a driveway.

Address One-mile stretch from Point Grey Road and McDonald to Point Grey Road and Alma | **Getting there** By car, parking available on First Avenue | **Hours** Unrestricted | **Tip** The home that yoga wear built, Chip Wilson's seaside mansion on the bike path, has topped the list of the most expensive homes in BC for five years in a row (3085 Point Grey Road, Vancouver, BC V6K 1A7). But don't expect to see too much, since most of it is hidden behind some tall hedges and a wall.

80 Punjabi Market
Epicentre of epic savours

If you need a new pashmina, colourful fabrics, or fancy some new jewellery, or you hunger for some authentic Indian culinary sensations, the Punjabi Market commercial district on Main Street between 47th and 51st Avenue, is the place to go. When you plan your visit, bring your shopping bags and an appetite. After browsing the shops, stop into a local restaurant or grocery store to satisfy your cravings and your curiosity with paneer, samosas, curry, naan, pakoras, candies, nuts, and spices while the sound of bhangra music completes the experience.

This unique cultural cluster of commerce in South Vancouver dates from the 1970s but can trace its roots back to the Kitsilano neighbourhood in 1908, when North America's first gurdwara, a place of worship for Sikhs, was built at 1866 West 2nd Avenue. Conveniently located near a source of much employment at the False Creek lumber mills, that first gurdwara was the cultural social point for the community and was even visited by India's first prime minister Jawaharlal Nehru (namesake of the 'nehru jacket') and his daughter Indira when they visited Vancouver in 1949. Had the lumber industry not moved south in the 1960s following the fire that destroyed much of the business in the False Creek area, perhaps Kitsilano would be home to the Punjabi Market today. But that was not to be. The lumber business did move toward mills along the Fraser River, and the labour force, the gurdwara, and economic and social momentum moved with it. Proceeds from the sale of the old gurdwara went toward building the massive new Ross Street Temple, which was opened on Vaisakhi Day (Sikh New Year) in 1970.

The connection between the Punjabi Market and the new Ross Street Temple becomes complete each April during the annual Vaisakhi Day Parade. The parade starts at the temple and circles up to 49th Avenue before making its way back to the temple.

Address Main Street, between 47th and 51st Avenues, Vancouver, BC V5X 3H3 | **Getting there** By car, street and metered parking is available on Main Street and side streets | **Hours** Unrestricted | **Tip** Visitors are welcome at the Sikh Temple (8000 Ross Street, Vancouver, BC V5X 4C5), designed by Vancouver architect Arthur Erickson in 1969. Look inside for the mosaic tile artwork of Guru Nanak, the first guru of Sikhism, which was part of the original gurdwara in Kitsilano.

81 Queen Elizabeth Park

Roam around the dome

Vancouverites enjoy some of the sunniest summers and gentlest winters anywhere in Canada, so no one who lives here can complain about the weather. But should you ever feel too cold or too wet, it's good to know there is something you can do to remedy the situation quickly: visit Queen Elizabeth Park and make your way to the Bloedel Conservatory.

Enter the doors of this impressive triodetic dome and immediately feel the warmth and humidity of the tropics on your skin. Fill your lungs with the sweet fresh air fed by 500 exotic plants and flowers, then listen to the squawks, chirps, tweets, and coos coming from the colourful parrots, pheasants, cockatoos, macaws, canaries, and finches that fill your ears and eyes with wonder.

While the scenes and sensations inside the conservatory dome are truly transformational, the parkland setting outside the dome is also special. For one thing, this is the highest point of land in Vancouver at 152 metres above sea level, and from here, you can enjoy unparalleled vistas of the city of Vancouver and the mountains. Near the conservatory, two amazing outdoor gardens are built into what used to be rock quarries in perhaps the most beautiful and original industrial site rehabilitation project you'll ever find. Then, there are over 1,500 trees representing every species of tree in Canada, a consequence of the park also being the country's first civic arboretum. Finally, there are several interesting statues and sculptures. The *Knife Edge Two Piece* is one of three copies of this abstract sculpture by famed British artist Henry Moore, the other two are in London and New York. A more whimsical work is J. Seward Johnson's 1984 statue called *Photo Session*. It is a life-sized statue of a man taking a picture of three friends, and also an amusing reminder of how it was done before mobile phones were invented.

Address 4600 Cambie Street, Vancouver, BC V5Z 2Z1, +1 (604) 873-7000, www.vancouver.ca/parks-recreation-culture/queen-elizabeth-park.aspx | **Getting there** By car, there is paid parking near the conservatory and free parking a short walk away | **Hours** Daily 10am–6pm | **Tip** The nearby restaurant Seasons In The Park has a fantastic menu and one of the most sensational views of Vancouver (Cambie and West 33rd Avenue, Vancouver, BC V5Y 2M4, www.vancouverdine.com/seasons).

82 Rainbow Crosswalk
Vancouver's pride

It should come as no surprise that a liberal, laid-back city like Vancouver can lay claim to Canada's first Rainbow Crosswalk. It was painted with pride at the intersection of Davie and Bute Streets and officially opened in 2013 by Tim Stevenson, Canada's first openly gay provincial cabinet minister. What makes this Rainbow Crosswalk even more interesting than just being the original one is the public plaza it leads to, and the diverse neighbourhood in which it's found.

The colourful, four-way crosswalk takes you into a small, square sanctuary surrounded by busy stores and apartments called Jim Deva Plaza. Jim was a community activist who founded the controversial Little Sister's Book and Art Emporium. The small bookstore became famous for a legal battle with the Canada Border Services Agency over the importation of what was alleged to be 'obscene materials' dealing with homosexuality. The case went all the way to the Supreme Court of Canada in 2000, and the small store won an historical landmark ruling. An informative, permanent sign explains Jim's lifetime passion of fighting for freedom of sexual expression. The Little Sister's Book and Art Emporium is still open, and it continues to assert his belief in free speech, as does the giant, turquoise, metal, speakers-corner-style megaphone sculpture in the plaza. The book store is just down the street from the Rainbow Crosswalk at 1283 Davie Street.

The plaza and crosswalk are the epicentre of Vancouver's vibrant gay community. Many of the businesses and residents along Davie Street fly the rainbow flag as a symbol of gay pride and bus stop benches and garbage cans are painted bright pink or in rainbow colours celebrating the city's long history of diversity. In this unique 'gaybourhood', you'll find an eclectic mix of interesting shops, gay-friendly bars, accommodations, and thriving nightlife.

Address Davie and Bute Streets, Vancouver, BC V6E 1N3 | Getting there By car, metered parking is available on Davie Street | Hours Unrestricted | Tip Not far from the crosswalk is the Pumpjack Pub, one of Vancouver's best gay nightspots. It opens at 1pm and usually stays open until 4 in the morning. Friday's are 'Jacked', featuring amateur dancers and strippers in an enclosed space on the dance floor (1167 Davie Street, Vancouver, BC V6E 1N2, www.pumpjackpub.com).

83 Raymond Burr's Grave

Final resting place of BC's first TV megastar

Perhaps best known for his iconic 1950s' television role as defence attorney Perry Mason, and undoubtedly one of the greatest TV stars of all time, Raymond Burr is British Columbia's first star of the big and small screens. He was an inspiring and groundbreaking ambassador for BC actors looking to make it big in Hollywood and New York. Every BC entertainer you can name – Seth Rogen, Ryan Reynolds, Jason Priestley, James Doohan, Michael J Fox, Dorothy Stratten, Bryan Adams, Sarah McLaughlin, Pamela Anderson, and others – all owe a debt of gratitude to Burr.

He dominated the airwaves in the 1940s, lending his distinctive and commanding deep voice to radio dramas like *Dragnet*. He appeared in over 50 feature films between 1946 and 1957 including the cult classic *Godzilla, King of the Monsters* and many epic film noir productions of that era. His role as creepy killer Lars Thorwald in Alfred Hitchcock's classic 1954 movie *Rear Window* with Jimmy Stewart and Grace Kelly is among his best bad guy performances. But it was his heroic TV roles as lawyer Perry Mason and then as detective Robert T. Ironside that enabled him to transcend from popular Hollywood actor into timeless cultural icon of the small screen.

The *Perry Mason* series first aired in 1957 and ran until 1966. It was quickly followed by *Ironside,* which ran from 1967 to 1975. During those two decades of pre-on-demand entertainment options, TV dominated pop culture, and Burr dominated TV. His performances and celebrity status earned him many industry accolades, including a prestigious star on Hollywood Boulevard. And yet, while that coveted brass star commemorates his career on the screen, it's this humble red marble grave marker in New Westminster that commemorates his life on our planet. Appropriately enough, Raymond Burr's grave is located in the 'Oddfellows' section of the cemetery.

Address 100 Richmond Street, New Westminster, BC V3L 4B3, +1 (604) 522-1323, www.newwestcity.ca/frasercemetery | Getting there By car, parking is available on Richmond Street | Hours Mon–Fri 7:30am–4pm | Tip Everyone has seen the Jack 'Gassy Jack' Deighton statue in Vancouver's Gastown district. But while you're at Fraser Cemetery, you can be among the few to visit his gravesite. Buried here in 1875, long before his legend grew, Deighton's grave was unmarked and nearly forgotten until local admirers remedied the situation in 1972 (www.gassyjack.com/links.html).

84 Reifel Bird Sanctuary
Down in bird land

The pursuit of studying and photographing birds is not called 'bird-watching', but rather 'birding'. Birders don't like being referred to as 'birdwatchers'.

That's good to know as you visit one of the best bird sanctuaries in Canada, located just 30 kilometres south of Vancouver on Westham Island. The sanctuary derives its name from its generous founder, George C. Reifel. He bought the 700 acres of land in 1927 and used it as a working farm for most of his life. In 1972, the Reifel family donated much of the land to the Federal Government under the conditions that it be turned into a retreat for birds and continue to bear the family name. It is somewhat ironic that a sanctuary for birds has a name that sounds identical to the word 'rifle', but it doesn't seem to make much difference to the millions of two-legged, winged creatures that visit the pristine marshlands every year.

Nearly 300 species of birds have been spotted at the sanctuary. A weekly species list is available to let you know which birds are in the sanctuary currently. You should bring your binoculars with you and wear comfortable walking shoes. Be prepared to walk through a network of flat gravel and grass trails alongside ponds and forested pathways that will take you by ever-changing coastal habitats and some amazing scenic lookouts. You can even climb up a 30-foot-tall observation tower.

Up to 100,000 snow geese arrive every fall from Wrangel island in Russia. Roughly half continue down to California, and the remainder winter on and near the sanctuary. Spring is a great time to observe the sandhill crane. They stand four feet tall with a distinctive bright red forehead. The small northern saw-whet owl is a favourite and eats small birds and rodents that it catches at night. On Sunday mornings, you can take an extremely interesting guided walk with an experienced birder as your 'wingman'.

Address 5191 Robertson Road, Delta, BC V4K 3N2, +1 (604) 946-6980,
www.reifelbirdsanctuary.com, bcsw@reifelbirdsanctuary.com | Getting there By car, follow
47A Avenue on to River Road West for three kilometres and then cross the bridge to
Westham Island. The main road on the other side of the bridge ends at the sanctuary. |
Hours Tue–Sun 9am–4pm | Tip In the summertime, the country road leading to the Reifel
Bird Sanctuary has several roadside vegetable stands and pick-your-own strawberry fields.
Small but well-stocked Keith's Produce has been around forever and is located just before
the Westham Island Bridge (3520 River Road West, Delta, BC V4K 3N2).

85 __ Rick Hansen Statue

A man in motion stays in motion

Motion and granite are two words that inherently contradict one another. But these words come together in a meaningful and historic way in a stunningly beautiful statue on the grassy slope behind the Vancouver General Hospital dedicated to Rick Hansen, Canada's inspirational Man in Motion.

To truly understand the meaning of this important civic monument to the concept of relentless, unstoppable motion, imagine the equator line that circles the globe. That line represents 24,901 miles and is the same distance that Rick travelled by wheelchair over a 26-month odyssey from 1985 to 1987 that took him through 34 different countries. Not only did he capture the imagination of all Canadians and people around the world on his Man in Motion World Tour, he also raised over 26 million dollars for spinal cord research and rehabilitation. Just as importantly, he demonstrated that anything is possible and taught the world to look beyond a person's disability. Since the tour, Rick's foundation has gone on to raise over $300 million dollars as he continues to strive for a more inclusive world where people with disabilities can live to their full potential.

One of Rick's greatest strengths is his razor-sharp focus on the future. The Rick Hansen Foundation (www.rickhansen.com) is responsible for other community-based programs, including the Barrier Busters initiative, an accessibility certification program, and a national school program that brings Rick's message to over 2,500 schools every day across Canada.

The larger-than-life statue is just a reminder of all the great work done and the hard work ahead. It's the creation of artist William Koochin, who captured what Rick looked like as he wheeled the equivalent of three marathons every day during his world tour. Take a close look at the statue and you'll still see Rick's eyes tirelessly looking into a more accessible future.

Address 818 West 10th Avenue, Vancouver, BC V5Z 1M9 | **Getting there** By car, hospital parking available at 850 West 12th Avenue | **Hours** Unrestricted | **Tip** There is a wonderful statue of Terry Fox, another iconic Canadian athlete, cancer activist, and overall hero from the same era, who was a friend of Rick Hansen. That statue is in front of BC Place Stadium (777 Pacific Boulevard, Vancouver, BC V6B 4Y8, www.bcplacestadium.com).

86 Rogers Arena
Three names, two bridges, one historic deal

The trend in big-city pro-sports arenas in the mid-1990s was to move them from the outskirts of town into the heart of the city. The old Pacific Coliseum, where the Canucks played since their inception in 1970, was located in a residential district in the far northeast corner of Vancouver. In order for Vancouver's NHL franchise to survive, it needed to build a brand new, state-of-the-art arena in the downtown core where it would be easy for people to attend games. At the time, however, large tracts of land big enough for a centrally-located hockey rink were practically non-existent. There was one potential spot sandwiched between a busy, twin-bridged, traffic viaduct. In the end, the arena was shoehorned into that tight spot, and it's one of the reasons why Rogers Arena has such fantastic sight lines for hockey games and concerts today.

When it opened, the arena was originally called General Motors Place. At the time, it was one of the first large naming-rights deals in the history of Canada. Just as important, and linked to the revenue generated through that sponsorship, the building was also the first and only modern major sports centre in Canada built exclusively with private money. Not a penny of taxpayer's dollars went into the $165 million arena. Since it opened in September 1995, over 25 million fans have enjoyed the steep seating and intimate views inside Rogers Arena.

The Vancouver Grizzlies spent six seasons playing basketball there before they moved to Memphis. Aside from General Motors Place, Rogers Arena has had one other official name. During the 2010 Winter Olympic Games, it was renamed Canada Hockey House due to regulations imposed by the IOC.

It's fun to walk around the outside of the building and observe its tight squeeze flush up against the Georgia Viaduct. But it is better to go inside for a game, concert, or a tour.

Address 800 Griffiths Way, Vancouver, BC V6B 6G1, +1 (604) 899-7400, www.rogersarena.com | Getting there SkyTrain to Stadium-Chinatown (Expo Line) | Hours Unrestricted from the outside; see website for event schedule | Tip In front of the arena (Abbott Street and Expo Boulevard, Vancouver, BC V5K 0A1) is a bronze statue of former Canucks President and General Manager Roger Neilson. It depicts him hanging a white towel over a hockey stick in a mock surrender during the 1982 Stanley Cup Playoffs.

87 Sam Kee Building
Queerest building in the whole dominion

That's how *The Daily World* described the Sam Kee Building in an article dated March 27, 1913. Nowadays, we'd just say it's strange. What makes the building so unusual is that it is a block long but only 4 feet 10 inches deep. It is truly one of the most unique commercial buildings in the world.

The building is a testament to creativity and a good tale about sticking it to the man. When the Sam Kee Company purchased a lot at this location in 1903, it was a standard-sized piece of property. But things changed when city planners decided to widen Pender Street. They made a deal to purchase land from Chang Toy, owner of the Sam Kee Company. Who knows if any malice was involved or not, but the city only compensated Toy for the part of the land they used, leaving him with a seemingly unusable slice of remaining space. Basically, Toy received a terribly unfair deal from the city. Maybe the city figured he'd just have to live with it. Undeterred, Toy decided to get the last laugh and hired architects to build a steel-framed building that not only used up the remaining five feet on the street level, but also extended the basement level under the sidewalk, and created a second floor that floats over the sidewalk too. The city may have figured they'd have a nice wide street with a little bit of unused green space on the side, but what they ended up with was a nice wide street with a commercial property adjacent to the sidewalk, underneath the sidewalk, and over the sidewalk as well.

City planners should have known it would be a mistake to try to cheat Chang Toy. He was one of the sharpest business entrepreneurs in the entire region. Born in China in 1857, Toy came to British Columbia when he was just 17. He started off as a labourer, but by the time he was 50, his company was making as much as $180,000 a year (about $5 million in today's money).

Address 8 West Pender Street, Vancouver, BC V6B 1R3 | Getting there By car, metered parking is available nearby | Hours Unrestricted from the outside only | Tip The Vancouver Chinatown Millennium Gate, just a few steps away, makes an iconic backdrop for a photo (26 West Pender Street, Vancouver, BC V6B 1R3).

88__ Science World Dome
Switched on since Expo 86

Modern downtown Vancouver has been shaped and defined by two seminal events. The 2010 Olympic Winter Games expedited the growth of the north side of False Creek. And 34 years earlier, the 1986 World's Exposition on Transportation and Communication, also known as Expo 86, developed the south side of False Creek.

One of the significant remnants from Expo 86 is today's Science World. The round, shiny sphere, which locals affectionately called the "giant golf ball," has become a Vancouver landmark. Its geodesic design was originated by the American author, designer, philosopher, inventor, and futurist Buckminster Fuller. It served as the Expo Center and welcomed over 22 million people who attended the 6-month event. Most of Expo 86's buildings were torn down, but Expo Center somehow avoided the wrecking ball. However, as the sun set every night for many years, the 17-story building faded into the shadows – until recently.

In 2023, Science World got a major lighting upgrade. Some of the old lights, including antiquated airplane lights, remained from the 1980s. Since it is one of the biggest geodesic domes in the world, a few strings of new holiday lights weren't going to do the trick. Instead, 651 state-of-the-art, bright, sparkling LED lights replaced the old system. That's three times the number of lights that the building had before, and 250 of those new lights actually face inwards, allowing them to reflect off of the dome's surface and provide even more effects, colours, and patterns than before. At almost $10 million, the price tag for the new lights was also a lot more than tree decorations.

The new, spectacularly coloured lights are activated in different imaginative ways each night. Today, Science World invites charities and nonprofits to apply to illuminate the building in their signature colours as a way of building awareness for their causes.

Address 1455 Quebec Street, Vancouver, BC V6A 3Z7, +1 (604) 443-7440, www.scienceworld.ca/visit-us/lights, info@scienceworld.ca | Getting there By car, parking is available at Lot 610 (1455 Quebec Street) | Hours Daily 10am–5pm | Tip The 60,000-seat BC Place stadium offers an amazing Northern Lights Display that lights up the other side of False Creek every night from sunset to 11pm and from sunrise to 6am on most days (777 Pacific Boulevard, Vancouver, BC V6B 4Y8, www.bcplace.com/the-stadium/the-roof/northern-lights-display).

89__Seaforth Armoury

Vancouver's Scottish baronial castle

Proclaimed 'the finest in the British Empire' when it was officially opened by Canada's governor general in 1936, the Seaforth Armoury is not only one of the city's most enduring architectural landmarks but home to Vancouver's storied infantry regiment the Seaforth Highlanders of Canada. Step inside the big blue doors facing Burrard Street during one of their public events and see the full history of the regiment on full display. The recent beneficiary of a multimillion-dollar structural renovation, the perimeter of the parade square now features historical exhibits from when the regiment was established in 1910 through to the present day. Among the most cherished items on display is the restored original Vimy Ridge memorial cross. Nearby is a display featuring the tail-end insignia from a Messerschmitt 109 shot down by a Seaforth soldier armed with a Bren gun.

The armoury also contains one of Vancouver's best-kept secrets: The Regimental Museum. Located on the second floor, the museum has lovingly preserved over 100 years of local military history including artefacts, paintings, photos, sculptures, trench art, and even furniture made by Vancouver's Highland soldiers.

Outside the armoury is one of BC's two Light Armoured Vehicle (LAV) memorials. The formerly-mobile memorial recognises the service and sacrifices of the roughly 500 members of the 39th Brigade (all the reserve units in British Columbia) who served in Afghanistan.

Photographs from the 1930s show that this was once a pastoral part of Vancouver. The iconic Molson brewery located next door, which often fills the air with the scent of barley and hops, did not arrive on the scene until the late 1950s. The luxury motor car showrooms that surround the place today were inconceivable futuristic fantasies when Lord Tweedsmuir officially opened the armoury over 80 years ago.

Address 1650 Burrard Street, Vancouver, BC V6J 3G4, +1 (604) 225-2520, www.seaforthhighlanders.ca | **Getting there** By car, metered street parking is available nearby | **Hours** By appointment; see website for public events | **Tip** Across the street, the Seaforth Peace Park contains a Sam Carter sculpture commemorating the bombing of Hiroshima and a Keith Shields sculpture of Hiroshima survivor Kinuko Laskey (1620 Chestnut Street, Vancouver, BC V6J 3K1).

90 _ Secret Climbing Tree
Legendary giant on a botanical boulevard

Who knows the origins of the legend of the secret climbing tree on Cambie Street? Was it local kids who first climbed up it decades ago and told all their closest friends? Or is it something that started more recently? Which tree is it, anyway? Is this a real thing or just an urban legend? The only way to know is to go and see for yourself.

Part of the tree's allure is its semi-secret location, but there's no doubt people just love to find a good climbing tree, and when they do, word gets out. In the past, this tree may have become too popular as various items have been squirrelled up its trunk to make it more comfortable or fun, like a hammock or a swinging rope. Other amateur arborists have countered with efforts to keep it au naturel and so the tree house type of paraphernalia has been stripped away.

This anonymous and unmarked tree is generally identified as an evergreen but is probably a giant sequoia (*Sequoiadendron giganteum*). The sequoia are well-known for both their girth and height and are sometimes even called 'the skyscrapers of the natural world'. The tallest sample in North America located in California reaches some 311 feet (95 metres) into the sky, while the tallest in nearby Queen Elizabeth Park measures 42 metres or 138 feet tall.

The secret climbing tree sits on an island of greenery separating the two lanes of Cambie Street which stretch from King Edward Street down to Southwest Marine Drive. This lush urban oasis, properly known as Cambie Heritage Boulevard, was created in the 1930s as part of a grand master plan for the city of Vancouver and contains some 450 trees. This early example of urban design and planning was influenced by the principles of the English Garden City movement and the ideals of the US City Beautiful movement.

Good luck finding the secret climbing tree and, when you do, please treat it kindly.

Address West King Edward Avenue and Cambie Street, Vancouver, BC V5Z 2X8 | Getting there SkyTrain to King Edward (Canada Line); by car, street parking is available along Cambie Street | Hours Unrestricted | Tip Seek out a tree of a different kind: Douglas Coupland's startling, golden, life-size reproduction of the Stanley Park's 800-year-old hollow tree (400 South West Marine Drive, Vancouver, BC V6P 6N6, www.coupland.com/public-arts/golden-tree).

91 The Shameful Tiki Room

For the tacky tourist in all of us

It rains a lot in Vancouver – it feels like all the time, especially in the winter, when grey, cold, wet skies are not recorded by days in a row but are tracked by months in a row. During that perennial soggy season, if you can't travel to Bali, Tahiti, or Hawaii, consider an hour or two escape from the drudgery at a hip Polynesian-style restaurant and bar that takes you back in time and transports you to a different climate. Shameful Tiki Room founder Rod Moore has created the perfect antithesis to our rainy malaise, beautifully replicating an old restaurant theme created in 1939 by the first Polynesian restaurant to open in America, a place called Don the Beachcomber in Hollywood. After its opening, a trend emerged which saw places with names like Trader Vic's, the Bali Hai, and Tiki Ti open up. Trader Vic's was a popular chain of restaurants, and Vancouver had one next to the old Bayshore Inn Hotel from 1961 to 1996. In a retro world where it's hip to be square, the Shameful Tiki Room opened its bamboo doors in 2013.

The food and drinks they serve are just plain old fun that never go out of style, like the Volcano Bowl that comes with straws for everyone at the table or the Blood of Kapu Tiki or the Mystery Bowl. While the more elaborate dishes are being served, the house lights dim, strobes and accent lighting replicate a storm, dry ice flows like lava, and the restaurant's sound system blasts out the sounds of tropical thunder.

The decorations are totally kitsch with lots of tacky souvenirs, thatched roofing, surf memorabilia, vintage posters, fish lamps, and old bottles. There are more rum-infused, multicoloured drinks with paper umbrellas and maraschino cherries than you can shake a palm leaf at. No light comes through the dining room windows, and there are even live exotic dancers. There is no shame in enjoying everything about this place.

Address 432 Columbia Street, Vancouver, BC V6A 2R8, +1 (604) 568-7273, www.theshopvancouver.com, brapp@theshopvancouver.com | Getting there By car, metered parking is available on Columbia Street | Hours Thu & Fri 1–5:30pm, Sat & Sun 1–4pm | Tip The Keefer Bar offers Asian-influenced small plate foods and specially crafted cocktails sure to cure whatever may be ailing you. It's just a short walk from The Shop (135 Keefer Street, Vancouver, BC V6A 1X3, www.thekeeferbar.com).

94_ Site of The Chicken Coop

Launchpad for the legendary Loretta Lynn

Vancouver isn't the first city that comes to mind when one thinks of places where American country music stars got their first big break. Normally, you'd imagine a club in Nashville, a radio station in Memphis, or maybe Gilley's honky tonk in Pasadena, Texas. But in Loretta Lynn's case, it was the most unlikely place of all: a backyard chicken coop in southeast Vancouver.

The story takes place when this part of town was still semi-agricultural. Ernest McGregor and his wife Irene Loranger had been living in a shack on the north arm of the Fraser River, saving up for an opportunity to buy land. When a nearby farm was sub-divided into residential lots, they jumped at the chance to build a home on Kent Avenue near the end of Elliott Street. That was 1949. A chicken coop came with the property and, since they liked music and dancing much better than chickens, the couple turned it into a makeshift dancehall. Ernest wired the place for sound, and the hoedowns became legendary. Enter budding record company executives Don Grashey and Chuck Williams. They had just started Zero Records and were looking for talent. One of their first artists was Sandi 'Shore' Loranger – Irene's niece. Sandi tells them about the good times at the Coop. Meanwhile, Loretta Lynn is living just 30 miles away in Custer, Washington. She's trying to get into the music business and she also hears about the Coop. She decides to come up and play a gig. At this point, fate intervenes. The label executives hear her perform and sign her. Within a year, Lynn's first record is made. She goes on to sell 45 million albums, write 24 hit singles, make 11 number one albums, and become the most awarded woman in country music. Ernest and Irene continued to live on Kent Avenue until the 1970s, but urban sprawl eventually consumed the chicken coop. Remarkably, their modest bungalow still survives.

Address 2541 East Kent Avenue, Vancouver, BC V5S 2H7 | Getting there By car, street parking is available on East Kent Avenue | Hours Unrestricted from the outside only | Tip The Fraser Shore Trail is across the street and affords excellent vistas of river traffic and echoes of the area's logging past. Walk east for about one kilometre and enjoy one of Vancouver's best burgers at Romers Burger Bar (8683 Kerr Street, Vancouver, BC V5S 0A4, www.romersburgerbar.com).

95 Southlands Riding Club

The horsey heart of Vancouver's urban agriculture

If you live in Vancouver, you can get a dog licence, and you can get a licence to keep chickens in your backyard. You can even have a bee-hive. But if you want to keep a horse at home, you've got to live in Southlands, the one area of the city where you'll definitely see more horses than bicycles.

Just 10 kilometres south of the city's downtown core and just north of the Fraser River, you'll find this unique, city-sanctioned, semi-agricultural enclave with special zoning laws that allow people to keep livestock at home. The area was one of the city's original agricultural areas, with the McCleery family establishing a 160-acre farm here in the 1800s, but its rural vibe was solidified in the 1940s when a few residents mounted up to form the Southlands Riding Club. Initially created to support the local polo-playing community, the club today is a non-profit society serving approximately 400 riding and non-riding members. The club hosts about 20 horse shows every year, and they're all free and open to the public. If you ever wanted to watch a polo game, a dressage event, jumping event, or maybe even figure out a way to get in the saddle yourself, this is the place to go. In addition to competitive and skills training, many of the club members just enjoy being outdoors and riding along the 50 kilometres of trails that extend up through Pacific Spirit Regional Park. Every Sunday, rain or shine, a dedicated group of riders go from stable to stable, and pasture to pasture, picking up riders as they mosey out along the trails.

The club is located east of the Point Grey Golf Club, west of the Marine Drive Golf Club, and next door to the public McCleery Golf Course. History buffs who also like to golf should make their way to the eleventh tee of the McCleery course where a bronze plaque marks the spot where Vancouver's first European-style residence once stood.

Address 7025 Macdonald Street, Vancouver, BC V6N 1G2, +1 (604) 263-4817, www.southlandsridingclub.com, info@southlandsridingclub.com | Getting there By car, parking is available and free at the riding club | Hours Mon–Fri 9am–5pm, Sat 8am–4pm | Tip The three-acre Southlands Heritage Farm is a great family destination in the area where kids can get up close to horses, ducks, chickens, goats, and sheep (6767 Balaclava Street, Vancouver, BC V6N 1R7, www.southlandsfarm.ca).

96 _ SS *Beaver* Wreck Cairn

Lasting tribute to the legendary steamship

Gordon Lightfoot never memorialised her wreck in song, as he did the *Edmund Fitzgerald*, but the SS *Beaver* holds a place in Canadian maritime history that is as colourful and storied as any ship could ever hope to have. As you walk up the path toward Prospect Point Lookout on the north end of Stanley Park, you will find this lonely stone cairn commemorating the day in 1888 when her travels came to an abrupt and inglorious end stuck upon the rocks below.

Today, there is almost nothing left of the wreck except some rusty nails and waterlogged splinters of the oak, elm, and teak which once formed her distinguished silhouette. The best artefacts, souvenirs, and remnants are more likely found in the Vancouver Maritime Museum or the Hastings Mill Store (see ch. 44) than in the foamy waves crashing among the rocks below. But when she first set sail from the Blackwall shipyard on London's famous River Thames in 1835, the copper-sheathed hull of this Hudson's Bay Company ship was fully equipped and prepared for adventure on the far edge of the British Empire.

Designed to be a steamship, she actually made her way from London to Vancouver by sail, and the two 35-horsepower steam engines were installed after she arrived at Fort Vancouver near present-day Portland, Oregon. In these days before the US-Canada border was established, before Oregon was a State, and before British Columbia even had official Colony status, the *Beaver* arrived in time to be both participant and witness to the economic, social, and political development of North America's Pacific West Coast.

In her life, she was a merchant ship and navy ship, and she carried everything from doorknobs to diplomats. But in her final days, beached and immobilised for five years, her carcass was slowly picked over by salvagers, souvenir hunters, and the elements until virtually nothing was left.

Address Near Prospect Point Lookout at Prospect Point, 5601 Stanley Park Drive, Vancouver, BC V6G 3E2 | Getting there By car, public parking is available at Prospect Point | Hours Unrestricted | Tip Enhance your trip with a side visit to the Prospect Point Restaurant and Deck, which includes an outdoor deck overlooking Lions Gate Bridge (5601 Stanley Park Drive, Vancouver, BC V6G 3E2, www.prospectpoint.com/dining).

97 _ St. Paul's Labyrinth
Pathway to peace

Tom Cochrane's hit song proclaimed that "life is a highway," and Paul McCartney wrote of the "long and winding road that leads to your door," but thousands of years before either of them put those thoughts to music, people of the far-distant past created labyrinths on the ground to help them explore their relationship with life, nature, and the world. In Vancouver, those seeking to contemplate life's many twists and turns can walk the path of enlightenment on the labyrinth located within St. Paul's Anglican Church.

The first of its kind in Canada, the Labyrinth at St. Paul's is a full 13-metre replica of the medieval labyrinth laid in the stone floor of the Cathedral de Notre-Dame de Chartres, the stunning Gothic cathedral located 60 miles south of Paris. While the original was built in 1201, this replica at St. Paul's was painted on the wooden floor of the gym's basketball court in 1997. Measuring some 12 metres across, the eleventh-circuit pattern looks small and compact but actually runs half a kilometre from start to finish. At the centre is a six-petal rose pattern where those shoeless souls walking the path can pause and reflect upon their journey. It is said that the labyrinth's design is based on sacred geometry, and that the 13-pointed star located underneath it ensures the balance and accuracy of the curves, spaces, and proportions.

Walking the path makes one realise that life truly is a highway of sorts, and it can also be a long and winding one. Sometimes it seems like we're going in circles, sometimes it seems we're farther away from our destination than when we started, sometimes it's a little disorienting. The journey is one you take on your own, one step at a time, but if you walk the labyrinth when others are there too it adds an interesting new dimension to the experience. Sometimes we're all on the same path, yet at times we appear to be going in opposite directions.

Address 1140 Jervis Street, Vancouver, BC V6E 2C7, +1 (604) 685-6832,
www.stpaulsanglican.bc.ca, info.labyrinth@stpaulsanglican.bc.ca | Getting there By car,
limited street parking available nearby and paid parking is available at the Advance
Parking (1237 Davie Street) | Hours Tue–Fri 8:30am–9:30pm, Sat 10am–noon, Sun
10am–noon, second and last Friday of every month 7–9pm | Tip Did you know
that the world's longest uninterrupted waterfront path is located in Vancouver? The
Seawall Path covers 28 kilometres (17 miles) from Spanish Banks to the Convention
Centre (www.vancouver.ca/parks-recreation-culture/seawall.aspx).

98 The *St. Roch*

RCMP sails the Northwest Passage

The crown jewels of England are guarded behind bullet-proof glass and locked up in a castle. The Constitution of the United States is preserved in a hermetically sealed titanium case. The *Mona Lisa* is roped off to make sure people keep their distance. All too often the most interesting treasures are displayed within sight but too far away to get a really good look. Not so at the Vancouver Maritime Museum. Here you can enjoy amazing artefacts of maritime history right up close. You can put your face mere inches away from Captain Vancouver's hand-drawn charts or have an up-close look at the chronometer he used on his exploration of the Pacific Rim in the 1790s. The original masthead from the famed CP ship *Empress of Japan* is here, as is the bell of the *Princess Sophia*, various remnants from the SS *Beaver* (see ch. 96), and more models of ships than you could imagine, including one made from pork bones by French prisoners of the Napoleonic Wars. In all there are some 15,000 objects and 100,000 images in the museum creating a veritable treasure chest of maritime memorabilia.

The anchor attraction of the museum is the Royal Canadian Mounted Police boat, the *St. Roch*. Don't get distracted wondering why the mounted police had a boat but focus instead on the ship's real claim to fame, which is that she was the first ship to successfully sail the Northwest Passage from west coast to east coast and also the first to circumnavigate North America. And don't just stand there, climb aboard! Have a peek at the crew quarters below decks, climb the ladder up to the wheelhouse and imagine what it would have been like to navigate this near century-old wooden vessel across the Arctic. Then take the steps down to the basement level of the museum and walk around the hull of the great ship. If you're not getting up close and personal at this museum, you're missing the boat.

Address 1905 Ogden Avenue, Vancouver, BC V6J 1A3, +1 (604) 257-8300, www.vancouvermaritimemuseum.com, info@vancouvermaritimemuseum.com | Getting there By car, closest paid parking is at 900 Chestnut Street; ferry to Maritime Museum | Hours Tue–Sun 10am–5pm | Tip Bring Fido along for a frolic at nearby Hadden Park Dog Beach (1000 Chestnut Street, Vancouver, BC V6J 3J9).

99 — Stanley Park Heron Nests
View the Heron Cam before you go

An uncommon but widespread bird in North America is the big majestic great blue heron. One-third of them worldwide live near Vancouver around the Salish Sea. They can weigh up to six pounds, are about four feet tall, and have a wingspan up to six feet. Herons live in groups of big nests called rookeries. Stanley Park has dozens of rookeries, mostly near the park's entrance.

Since 2001, many herons have been nesting behind the low-rise stone Parks Board office building at 2099 Beach Avenue, making it the largest urban great blue heron colony in North America.

The first sighting of these birds in Stanley Park dates back to 1929. Back then, powerful binoculars would have been considered high tech. Today, there is a new option to assist in viewing great blue herons. The popularity of the rookery prompted the Parks Board to install a high-definition 'Heron Cam' in 2015, which live streams a view high atop a tree into the inside of a nest. Through the online camera, you can now watch the birds' courtship and mating rituals, see their nest-cleaning habits, and, if your timing is right, you can even witness little chicks hatching. Online or in person from the street below you can also see the little baby herons' parents fending off predators like the eagles and raccoons that also live in Stanley Park. When you see them flying, you'll be awe-inspired by their graceful and slow wingbeats.

The heron's unique location near the Parks Board makes one think that these prehistoric-looking flying dinosaurs may be smarter than we think. The elected board is of course the civic governing body under whose purview the birds fall. Being classified as a species 'at risk' in BC, it's a good thing the great blue herons live near their authoritative guardians.

The Heron Cam streams from the beginning of March till the end of the summer breeding season.

Address 2099 Beach Avenue, Vancouver, BC V6G 1Z4, www.stanleyparkecology.ca/conservation/urban-wildlife/herons | **Getting there** By car, paid parking available in the Parks Board Office lot on Park Lane | **Hours** Unrestricted | **Tip** Behind their tree in the park, the herons have a bird's-eye view of the Stanley Park Lawn Bowling Club. Not only is it over 100 years old but it is also the largest lawn bowling club in Canada (9100 Stanley Park Drive, Vancouver, BC V6G 3E2, www.splbc.com).

100__Stir Coffee House

Old-fashioned values with a pinch of hipness

At the entrance to the old historic village of Ladner stands an odd-shaped triangular block where back in 1963 a local proprietor named Johnny Lowe opened a neighbourhood grocery store on what came to be known as Johnny's Corner. His store served as a focal point that helped draw the community together. Today, Johnny's son Rob has followed in his dad's footsteps of enriching the community by converting the old store into one of the best cafés in Greater Vancouver.

Stir Coffee House has an ever-changing, always interesting display of local photographers' art on its walls, and it sources its tea, coffee, baked goods, sweet honey, and other supplies locally. A turntable behind the front counter spins an eclectic mix of LPs, and a handmade wooden book box that sits outside the shop serves as a great resource where residents and visitors drop off and pick up used books. In the summertime, the outdoor patio is an unrushed place to sit down and read.

The corner's history goes back even further than the early 1960s though, and in the lobby of a small joining office building, you'll find a great black-and-white interpretive photographic display. Reading it, you'll learn more about the small farming and fishing community of Ladner. It is interesting to note all the different enterprises that have occupied the corner since the first commercial building was erected in there in 1902. It started out as a blacksmith shop, went on to become a bicycle and lawnmower repair depot, was once a showroom for farm implements and machinery, and was also a coffee shop in the late 1950s.

Today, the coffee still pours hot but the shop is still very hip, where young, enthusiastic, and energetic baristas serve up delicious beverages in old-fashioned, turquoise mugs. One thing that hasn't changed is the sense of community the old corner has bolstered for over 100 years.

Address 101-5085 48th Avenue, Ladner, BC V4K 1W1, +1 (604) 940-8005, www.stircoffeehouse.com | Getting there By car, street parking is available on 48th Avenue | Hours Mon–Fri 7am–4:30pm, Sat & Sun 8am–4:30pm | Tip On the other side of 47A Avenue is a small strip of greenery that runs adjacent to an important slough. This is the civic oasis called Magee Park that has a few nice benches where you can watch ducks swim by as you sip your coffee (4740 Arthur Drive, Ladner, BC V4K 2X5).

101 __ The Storybook House
Stratford-upon-Vancouver

Although roofs are meant to keep out water, one atop an expensive West Side Vancouver home has been designed to look like water. More accurately, to look like artistic waves breaking over an open ocean. The home, not far from Jericho Beach, has a rare Sea Wave Roof. The rest of the home has some additional unique design features that make it stand out while adding an old-world charm to the heavily treed neighbourhood.

Vancouver has two or three of these quirky, rare architectural gems and they are referred to as 'storybook houses'. Technically, this style of home is called Provincial Revivalism. Both terms describe a style of architecture and roofing that is a cross between an old fairy tale-like European cottage and something out of a Walt Disney cartoon. These homes were popular from the 1920s to the early 1940s, mainly on the West Coast of North America, and particularly in Los Angeles. There are no hard and fast rules for just what makes a storybook house a storybook house. However, the main features are an intentionally uneven roof that looks thatched and an overall playful and whimsical look.

Today, this type of roof is very expensive to build and that's partly why these homes are so rare. They are made out of steam-bent cedar shingles, and the process of layering the shingles in a thick and undulating manner is very labour intensive. If fact, it is so labour intensive and impractical that it is quickly becoming a lost art.

The 2,500-square-foot bungalow was inspired by the childhood Tudor-style cottage of Shakespeare's wife Anne Hathaway near Stratford-upon-Avon in England.

This house is definitely fun to look at. Standing far enough away from the roof, you can study its humble and beautiful imperfections while being transported back in time. While you're admiring the home, don't be surprised if Bilbo Baggins sneaks out the back door.

Address 3979 West Broadway, Vancouver, BC V6R 3V4 | **Getting there** By car, street parking available | **Hours** Unrestricted from the outside only | **Tip** If this type of roof design interests you, there is one other great example in the city (587 West King Edward Avenue, Vancouver, BC V5Z 2C4), where another old house with its beautiful wavy roof intact has been incorporated into a new modern multi-unit townhouse development.

102___The Sylvia Hotel

A cat, some ivy, and a colourful Hungarian baroness

One of Vancouver's most beloved and classic institutions is the Sylvia Hotel. For over 100 years, the eight-story landmark has sat ageing gracefully on the shores of English Bay. The Virginia creeper ivy that completely covers the Gilford Street side of the hotel today only softens the stately old gal's appearance. That ivy was planted shortly after the hotel opened in 1913 by one of the building's first tenants, who lived there for 25 years.

Constructed in 1912, the Sylvia was originally built to be an apartment building. It was designed by Seattle architect W. P. White for Mr Abraham Goldstein, who named the building after his eldest daughter. At the time, the Sylvia cost $250,000 to build.

The Sylvia was the first pet-friendly hotel in Vancouver. With the massive and bucolic Stanley Park right next door, there couldn't be a better location for pets to run around, and there is one legendary cat that became famous by overstaying his welcome. In the early 1990s, a stray cat wandered into the lobby of the Sylvia Hotel, and the manager at the time said, "That cat's got to go as soon as it stops raining." Well, the cat didn't go, and it ended up staying for seven years as the hotel's official mascot. The cat soon adopted the name Mr Got to Go, and since then, three popular children's books have been written about him. The books are for sale in the hotel lobby where you will also find pictures and artefacts about the four-legged feline freeloader.

Another offbeat story involves a Hungarian baroness from Manhattan who stayed in the Sylvia Hotel every summer for a dozen years in the 1950s and 1960s and always resided in room 727. On one hot August afternoon, the hotel's management threatened to evict her for allegedly tossing grapes out of her window and trying to hit the pedestrians on Beach Avenue below. So watch for flying fruit as you round the corner onto the entrance on Gilford.

Address 1154 Gilford Street, Vancouver, BC V6G 2P6, +1 (604) 681-9321, www.sylviahotel.com, info@sylviahotel.com | Getting there By car, paid parking available in underground lot below the hotel | Hours Lobby hours; see website for restaurant hours | Tip Just around the corner from the hotel is tiny Morton Park, featuring 14 enormous bronze statues that look like half-naked, laughing Buddhas. They were meant to be a temporary display when they went up in 2009 as part of the Vancouver Biennale. The $1.5-million statues had the last laugh though – they are still there (1800 Morton Avenue, Vancouver, BC V6G 1V3).

103 — Tsawwassen Terminal

Fantastic ferry flotilla

North America's second-biggest island is nestled in the Pacific Ocean less than 50 miles from Vancouver. In 1960, the BC government devised a system to shuttle people, cars, and trucks back and forth between these two points. BC Ferries has grown since then to be the planet's largest ferry fleet, carrying a staggering 23 million passengers and over 8 million cars per year on 34 different vessels. The one thing the ships have in common is they are almost all painted white.

The epicentre of the system is the Tsawwassen Ferry Terminal 40 minutes from Downtown Vancouver. The First Nations' word *tsawwassen* means 'land facing the sea'. At this busy hub, you can purchase what is surely the best transportation value on the Pacific Ocean. For less than $20, you can board one of these massive ships to enjoy an ocean cruise without having to bring a suitcase. The sailing to Victoria boasts some of the most spectacular craggy and rugged coastline scenery in the world. Don't be surprised if the ferry's captain announces, "Ladies and Gentlemen, a pod of killer whales can be seen on the ships' starboard side." Sightings of whales, eagles, and otters are common. The amazing, supernatural beauty of the windswept inlets and narrow saltwater passages can distract you from the ships' great inside amenities. Three comfortable passenger decks with massive windows have all the restaurants, coffee, and gift shops offered by luxury cruise lines. But instead of being at sea for 7 days, your cruise is 90 minutes.

The terminal is named after the West Coast First Nations' Tsawwassen Band, which owns the surrounding land. Some of the ferries have graphics and motifs depicting traditional aboriginal art, and others have large colourful sports murals created for the Vancouver 2010 Olympic Winter Games. Venture out to the Tsawwassen Ferry Terminal simply to watch the ferries come and go.

Address 1 Ferry Causeway, Tsawwassen Ferry Terminal Delta, Vancouver, BC V6C 0B9, +1 (888) 223-3779, www.bcferries.com | Getting there By car, parking is available at Impark | Hours See website for hours | Tip The BC Ferries Experience Card offers fare discounts on 15 ferry routes in the system. Available at any ferry ticket booth.

104 Twin Urinals

Urine for a surprise at Heritage Hall

When men pee, it is generally a solitary activity. Most of their attention is directed toward the matter in hand, so to speak. Occasionally, distractions such as a conversation with a neighbouring urinal-mate may break out. But always their steely glance remains directed to the wall inches in front of him. However, there is one really old weird urinal in Vancouver that contradicts that time-honoured convention. It is in the old Heritage Hall building that went up in 1915, and it is a double urinal designed for men to pee eye-to-eye.

Who came up with such an outlandish idea as a twin urinal? John Shanks did, that's who (he was from Europe, a you're-a-peein', if you will). Shanks was the founder of Shanks & Co. Ltd. of Barrhead, Scotland. He was alive from 1826 to 1895, an era when sanitary waste disposal systems were extremely important because of the prevalence of waterborne diseases such as typhus and cholera. The double urinal was just one of his patents, and Shanks had a hundred others. One of his 'twin tinklers' ended up in the Heritage Hall in Vancouver, and it has been helping to relieve men two-at-a-time for over 100 years.

The Heritage Hall is one of the oldest buildings in Vancouver. It's a beautiful, nearly square, three-story structure full of lavish, 19th-century-style ornamentation and beautiful stonework. Many Vancouver residents think that it used to be a city hall, a church, or a bank, but they are all wrong. It was originally a post office, then a federal agriculture building, and from 1965 to 1976, it was an RCMP headquarters. At that time, Canada's National Police Force was dominated by men, and the urinal would have only increased the force's efficiency. Today the Heritage Hall contains several not-for-profit offices, and its ballroom is available for private and community functions. Although it's not open to the public, it can often be accessed for a small donation at weekend craft fairs, vinyl record sales, comic book swaps, and art exhibitions.

Address 3102 Main Street, Vancouver, BC V5T 3G7, www.heritagehall.bc.ca, heritage@heritagehall.bc.ca | Getting there By car, metered parking is available on Main Street | Hours See Heritage Hall's Facebook page for public events. | Tip Vancouver has 10 public, self-cleaning toilets. A nearby facility at the corner of Davie and Bute is there when you need it (Davie and Bute Streets, Vancouver, BC V6E 1N, vanmapp1.vancouver.ca/gmaps/covmap.htm?map=public_toilet&zoom=14).

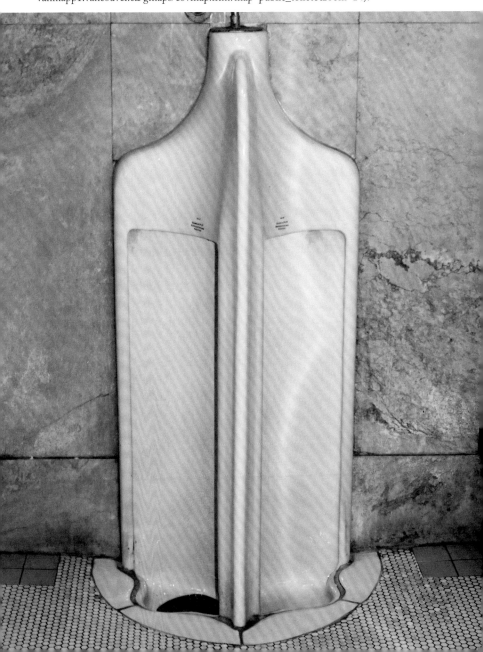

105__UBC Rose Garden

They paved paradise and put up a rose garden

UBC Rose Garden is one of the most beautiful vistas in Vancouver. Gaze out over the rose garden and fill your senses with an ocean view, a never-ending panorama of mountains that fade into the distance, and the smell of over a dozen varieties of roses. Cleverly located on top of a parking garage – such a Vancouver thing to do – this uncommon campus cornucopia of colour is built on the site of the original 1949 rose garden that stood here until construction of the nearby Chan Centre began in 1995. Perhaps heeding Joni Mitchell's warning about paving paradise to put up a parking lot, the university found a way to put in a parking lot and keep the rose garden. It was designed by landscape architects Perry & Associates and reopened to the public in 1997.

You don't need rose-coloured glasses to appreciate the ways in which this garden inspires the soul and the senses. There are over 150 species of roses, which fossil evidence suggests have been on the planet for over 35 million years. But when you walk among the buds and petals that form this sensual oasis, you'll be soaking in the sights and scents of mostly hybrid tea and floribunda roses. What the experience will mean is up to you but consider that roses have meant so much to so many people over the ages. From the days of the Roman Empire, through the War of the Roses, to today's ubiquitous tattoo parlours, roses have captured the imagination and have been steeped in meaning and symbolism. Roses also appear on four tarot cards: the fool, the magician, strength, and death. Even the colours of roses have meaning from celebrating love to lamenting death.

Easily one of the most Instagramable places in the city, the rose garden has been the backdrop in thousands of convocation pictures and who knows how many weddings. So when you visit, be sure to bring a camera. But don't worry about finding a place to park.

Address 6301 Crescent Road, Vancouver, BC V6T 1Z2, www.maps.ubc.ca/PROD/
index_detail.php?locat1=N026 | Getting there By car, park at the Rose Garden Parkade
off Northwest Marine Drive | Hours Unrestricted | Tip The nearby Chan Centre is one
of the finest performance venues in Canada. Schedule your visit to an upcoming concert
or lecture (6265 Crescent Road, Vancouver, BC V6T 1Z1, www.chancentre.com).

106__ Vancouver Police Museum

Home of the Kosberg family murder axe

Surely one of the more gruesome artefacts at the Vancouver Police Museum is the double-headed axe used by 16-year-old Thomas Kosberg to murder six members of his family. His mother, father, two brothers, and two sisters were all drugged and then hacked to death in their beds. Miraculously, six-month-old baby Osborne was spared. The deadly event took place at the family home on Main Street and East 22nd Avenue early on the morning of December 10, 1965, and it remains one of the most shocking and horrific crimes in Vancouver history. Shortly after the murders, Thomas propped this axe up against the kitchen stove, left the house, and turned himself in to his psychiatrist. Look closely at the axe now, and you can still see a blond hair clinging to the blade.

Stories and artefacts like this abound at the Vancouver Police Museum. If you're a fan of criminal history or want to learn more about the darker side of Vancouver, the museum has enough murder weapons, authentic gangster mug shots, police records, unsolved mysteries, counterfeit banknotes, drug paraphernalia, illegal weapons, and contraband to keep you amused for quite some time. Skull casts of the 1940s'-era unsolved 'babes in the woods' murders can be seen up close, along with the hatchet that was used to slay the still unknown brothers. The gun display includes samples of weapons used by good guys and bad guys alike. There are a few tommy guns of the type used by Al Capone and other gangsters and a variety of pistols including the notorious Walther PPK, James Bond's weapon of choice. If you've never seen a human skull with a bullet hole in it or if you want to know what a stab wound to the heart looks like, you've come to the right place. The recreated morgue area features a couple of stainless-steel autopsy tables as well as some fascinating biological samples preserved in jars.

Address 240 East Cordova Street, Vancouver, BC V6A 1L3, +1 (604) 665-3346, www.vancouverpolicemuseum.ca, info@vancouverpolicemuseum.ca | **Getting there** By car, metered parking is available on East Cordova Street | **Hours** Thu–Sat 11am–5pm, Sun noon–5pm | **Tip** Look carefully at the masonry on the exterior of the neoclassical Vancouver Art Gallery and you'll see the word *Police* carved into the granite above one of the doorways, as these were the Vancouver Law Courts from 1911 to 1979 (750 Hornby Street, Vancouver, BC V6Z 2H7, www.vanartgallery.bc.ca).

107__ Visions of Possibilities
Building accessibility and rebuilding lives

The first thing you see as you enter the Blusson Centre is the perfect balance of a modern accessible design combined with a beautiful artistic metaphor. The sleek metal-and-glass building located behind the Vancouver General Hospital is the world's largest facility dedicated to spinal cord research and patient care. Opened in 2008, it is also one of the world's most accessible buildings.

The Blusson Centre's striking, three-story wheelchair ramp poetically communicates the centre's aspirations. Ever onward, ever forward, ever upward. At the same time, it serves as a practical and accessible pathway into the building. It's over 200 metres long with a five percent incline, and every 10 metres the ramp has a level spot to further aid in its ease and accessibility.

Canadian hero and wheelchair athlete Rick Hansen (see ch. 85) pulled together the different private and government stakeholders that made the Blusson Centre possible. Thanks to his leadership, thousands of individuals can receive treatment and support and exchange ideas.

The Blusson Centre is also a place where hundreds of researchers and clinicians work to solve one of the most devastating healthcare challenges: paralysis from spinal cord injury as a result of sudden trauma, such as a car crash, fall, or illness.

World-renowned local mouth-painting artist Robb Dunfield sustained a fall that left him paralysed from the neck down and ventilator dependent when he was only 18 years old. One of Robb's paintings, *Visions of Possibilities,* a six-by-eight-foot portrait of his daughters playing at the beach, is proudly displayed at the centre's entrance. The size and grandeur of Robb's painting serves as an example of what is possible when you have a dream. The building itself is a testament to Rick Hansen's dream to remove barriers and accelerate progress to find a cure for paralysis after spinal cord injury.

Address 818 West 10th Avenue, Vancouver, BC V5Z 1M9, +1 (604) 875-4992 | Getting there By car, metered parking available across the street | Hours Mon–Fri 7:30am–6pm | Tip 10th Avenue is one of the busiest bike corridors in Vancouver with over 500,000 people cycling on it every year. If you want to join the accessible throng of cyclists, there is a Mobi Bike Rental spot a block from the Blusson Centre (West 10th Avenue and Oak Street, Vancouver, BC V6H 3Z6, www.mobibikes.ca).

108_Waterfront Station

Timeless terminal of temporal travellers

Most people travelling through Waterfront Station were just passing through. But, since this is regarded as the most haunted building in Vancouver, it is clear that some travellers have preferred to stay.

The most famous ghost is the train operator who fell on the tracks and became decapitated. You can understand why he might have trouble moving on. But since the station opened in 1914, unknown millions have passed through this pacific terminal of the transcontinental Canadian Pacific Railway.

While it seems as though it must have been the CPR's first train station in the area, it is in fact the third. They really seemed to enjoy building train stations. The first one was in Port Moody, which only lasted 10 years before they built the second one at the end of Granville Street one block further west of this location. That station lasted 15 years until Waterfront Station finally seemed to be the end of the line for train station architects. The building was built to impress as it was the endpoint for many transcontinental travellers who might have worried – as they trundled for days across the wide-open prairies and through the rugged Rocky Mountains – that they were leaving the comforts of sophisticated urban civilisation behind for good.

Disembarking the train from Montreal or Toronto, travellers would have been comforted and awed by the stunning white Ionic-style columns that decorate the neoclassical exterior and impressed by the scenic Canadian landscape paintings that decorate the building's interior.

These original paintings were done by Adelaide Langford, an artist of sufficient calibre that one of her paintings was once included in the collection of the royal family. The location of the paintings, somewhat hidden high upon the station walls, has preserved them as some of the best last remaining original railway station paintings in the country.

Address 601 West Cordova Street, Vancouver, BC V6B 1G1, +1 (604) 953-3333, www.thecanadaline.com/station-guides/waterfront | Getting there SkyTrain or Seabus to Waterfront (Canada & Expo Line); by car, paid parking available at Impark lot at Granville Square and PWC Place | Hours Unrestricted | Tip Outside the station, take a moment to appreciate the poignant and sublime bronze *Angel of Victory* statue. The status was designed by artist Coeur de Lion MacCarthy in 1922 to honour the 1,100 CPR employees who died in World War I.

109 Westham Island Bridge

Lumber and leverage in Ladner

Not much has changed since 1910, when a 1,066-foot crossing was completed, connecting the small fishing and farming village of Ladner with the canneries and berry fields on Westham Island. Back then, teams of plow horses could be seen making their way across the bridge along with the occasional slow-moving, rudimentary tractor chugging its way to market with fresh produce in tow. The bridge took three years to construct out of local materials and made a huge difference to the young, growing community. It meant that farmers could save time and money not having to rely on the small ferry that was the only link to the mainland at the time.

The fact that the Westham Island Bridge is a swing bridge makes it just that much more storied and interesting. Up until 1971, when an electric motor was installed, the bridge operator would manually use a really long metal lever and push it in a clockwise direction with all the leverage he could muster to open the span for fishing and pleasure boats leaving the Fraser River tidal estuary for the nearby ocean. The small shack on the west side of the bridge where the operator was stationed stands there to this day. If it is not remarkable enough that this huge bridge was moved by one man, it gets more mind-boggling when you learn that the operator had only one arm and did the strenuous manual task several times a day until he retired at the age of 71.

Today, birders from all over the world cross the historic bridge to visit the Reifel Bird Sanctuary (see ch. 85), and Vancouverites use it to make their way to the pick-your-own berry farms on Westham Island, along with the occasional still slow-moving farm vehicle.

As you might expect, a bridge this picturesque and historic makes for a natural film location. One of the most famous episodes of the TV series *The X-Files* called "The Kill Switch" was filmed on location on the bridge.

Address Near the intersection of Westham Island Road and Kettles Road, Ladner, BC V4K 3N2 | Getting there By car, the bridge is three kilometres west of Ladner, follow 47A Avenue onto River Road and look for the bridge on the right. Parking on the side of the road. | Hours Unrestricted | Tip Just before the bridge is Wellington Point Park, with a fortified wooden pier that offers great views of some interesting fish processing plants and dozens of houseboats on the river (3653 River Road West, Ladner, BC V4K 3N2).

110 Wing Sang Building

Chinatown history meets contemporary art

Stand outside this exquisitely restored 1899 structure and try to imagine what it was like when the concrete sidewalk beneath your feet was nothing more than a series of wooden planks, and the asphalt-paved street was nothing but mud and dirt. If you can do that, you can begin to understand what a grand building it was in its day. It is remarkable for what it was when built, and for the story behind the man who built it.

Yip Sang was born in China in 1845 and arrived in California in 1864. Like many young men seeking their fortunes, he tried many things and visited many places before settling down and making it big in Vancouver. His résumé included time as a cowboy, a gold prospector, dishwasher, cook, and door-to-door coal salesman. Everything changed for Sang when the Canadian Pacific Railway came to town. His fluency in English and Chinese, his status as a naturalised British subject, and his savvy business skills landed him a job as a bookkeeper with the railway. Before long, he was overseeing a workforce of thousands. Eventually, Sang made enough money to branch out on his own. From the Wing Sang building, the first brick building in Chinatown, he oversaw a business empire that included real estate investments, labour contracting, and importing and exporting goods to China. He also imported and processed opium – entirely legal at the time – which makes this building one of the oldest drug factories in town. By 1908, his company was one of the largest in the city with real estate worth over $200,000, and Yip Sang became noted as one of Vancouver's most successful entrepreneurs.

Today, the Wing Sang Building stands proudly as the oldest building in Chinatown and home to one of Canada's largest contemporary art collections. The restoration of the building, and the inclusion of the art collection, is the work of noted Vancouver condo developer Bob Rennie.

Address 51 East Pender Street, Vancouver, BC V6A 1S9, +1 (604) 682-2088, www.renniecollection.org | Getting there By car, metered parking is available nearby | Hours See website | Tip The neoclassical BC Electric Railway Terminal is another historic Vancouver building just around the corner from the Wing Sang Building (425 Carrall Street, Vancouver, BC V6B 6E3).

111 Wooden Roller Coaster
Shake, rattle, and roll

When it comes to roller coasters, there are two kinds: metal and wooden. The metal ones are generally sleek, fast, and modern. The wooden ones are rickety, bumpy, and noisy. Timber roller coasters are also usually older, more interesting, and more fun to ride.

That's about all you need to know about roller coasters to appreciate that Vancouver boasts one of the most famous roller coasters in North America. Since 1958, it has sat near the corner of Cassiar and Hastings Streets on the grounds of the Playland at the Pacific National Exhibition. The ride has a world-class reputation amongst coaster connoisseurs for having lots of hills, fast turns, and a bone-rattling, horrifying, 75-foot drop at its start. It's a real classic and has been awarded landmark status by the American Coaster Enthusiast (ACE) organisation.

That initial drop is what powers the eight-car coaster for the entire 2,840-foot ride at speeds of up to 45 miles per hour. Unlike metal roller coasters, wooden ones feel really, really unsafe. For the entire thrilling, 90-second ride, it feels and sounds like you are careening out of control. The adrenaline-pumping inertia around the dozens of corners slams you into the small metal safety bar with so much G-force you'll feel like an astronaut on the space shuttle. But not to worry – the roller coaster is perfectly safe. There has not been a major accident reported in its 60 years of operation. Properly maintained wooden roller coasters never really die, and Vancouver's coaster has a small crew that works on it year-round, replacing wooden beams, lubricating bearings, and overhauling seals and fasteners. Rest assured, you'll live to tell your friends about the experience.

For the real speed freaks, purchase an all-day pass for all the rides at Playland. In 1958, you could have ridden the wooden roller coaster for a mere 40 cents.

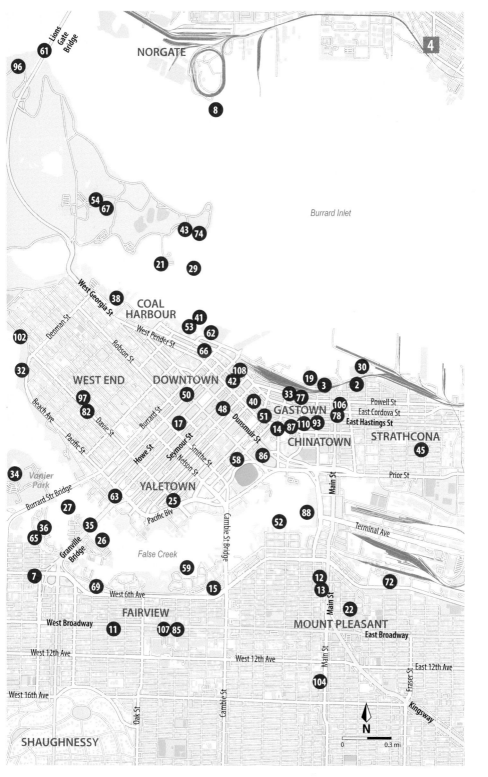

Dave Doroghy, Graeme Menzies
111 Places in Victoria
That You Must Not Miss
ISBN 978-3-7408-1720-6

Dave Doroghy, Graeme Menzies
111 Places in Whistler
That You Must Not Miss
ISBN 978-3-7408-1046-7

Jennifer Bain, Liz Beddall
111 Places in Ottawa
That You Must Not Miss
ISBN 978-3-7408-1388-8

Jennifer Bain, Christina Ryan
111 Places in Calgary
That You Must Not Miss
ISBN 978-3-7408-0749-8

Elizabeth Lenell-Davies,
Anita Genua, Claire Davenport
111 Places in Toronto
That You Must Not Miss
ISBN 978-3-7408-0257-8

Harriet Baskas, Cortney Kelley
111 Places in Seattle
That You Must Not Miss
ISBN 978-3-7408-1992-7

Katrina Nattress, Jason Quigley
111 Places in Portland
That You Must Not Miss
ISBN 978-3-7408-0750-4

Floriana Petersen, Steve Werney
111 Places in San Francisco
That You Must Not Miss
ISBN 978-3-7408-2058-9

Floriana Petersen, Steve Werney
111 Places in Silicon Valley
That You Must Not Miss
ISBN 978-3-7408-1346-8

Laurel Moglen, Julia Posey,
Lyudmila Zotova
111 Places in Los Angeles
That You Must Not Miss
ISBN 978-3-7408-1889-0

Brian Joseph
111 Places in Hollywood
That You Must Not Miss
ISBN 978-3-7408-1819-7

Kelsey Roslin, Nic Yeager,
Jesse Pitzler
111 Places in Austin
That You Must Not Miss
ISBN 978-3-7408-1642-1

Dana DuTerroil, Joni Fincham,
Daniel Jackson
111 Places in Houston
That You Must Not Miss
ISBN 978-3-7408-1697-1

Dana DuTerroil, Joni Fincham,
Sara S. Murphy
111 Places for Kids in Houston
That You Must Not Miss
ISBN 978-3-7408-1372-7

Philip D. Armour, Susie Inverso
111 Places in Denver
That You Must Not Miss
ISBN 978-3-7408-1220-1

Cristyle Egitto, Jakob Takos
111 Places in Palm Beach
That You Must Not Miss
ISBN 978-3-7408-1695-7

Brian Hayden, Jesse Pitzler
111 Places in Buffalo
That You Must Not Miss
ISBN 978-3-7408-1440-3

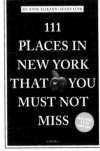

Jo-Anne Elikann, Susan Lusk
111 Places in New York
That You Must Not Miss
ISBN 978-3-7408-1888-3

Wendy Lubovich, Ed Lefkowicz
111 Museums in New York
That You Must Not Miss
ISBN 978-3-7408-0379-7

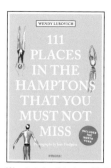

Wendy Lubovich, Jean Hodgens
111 Places in the Hamptons
That You Must Not Miss
ISBN 978-3-7408-1891-3

Kim Windyka, Heather Kapplow,
Alyssa Wood
111 Places in Boston
That You Must Not Miss
ISBN 978-3-7408-1558-5

Andréa Seiger, John Dean
111 Places in Washington
That You Must Not Miss
ISBN 978-3-7408-1890-6

Brandon Schultz, Lucy Baber
111 Places in Philadelphia
That You Must Not Miss
ISBN 978-3-7408-1376-5

Allison Robicelli, John Dean
111 Places in Baltimore
That You Must Not Miss
ISBN 978-3-7408-1696-4

Amy Bizzarri, Susie Inverso
111 Places in Chicago
That You Must Not Miss
ISBN 978-3-7408-1030-6

Michelle Madden, Janet McMillan
111 Places in Milwaukee
That You Must Not Miss
ISBN 978-3-7408-1643-8

Sandra Gurvis, Mitch Geiser
111 Places in Columbus
That You Must Not Miss
ISBN 978-3-7408-0600-2

Acknowledgements

Good people know good stories. We are both fortunate to know a lot of good people who gave us suggestions, leads, and, most importantly, their encouragement to complete this book:

Cheryl Ellis, Jeff Veniot, David Kincaid, Kevin Bowers, Miriam Soet, Ray McAllister, Rick Hansen, Gary Cadman, Pat Browne, Mariko Nakagawa, Brian Antonson, Andrea Kwiatkowsky, Baird Menzies

Special thanks to Karen Seiger, a long distance runner herself, who was there at the starting line with us, helped us over the hills, and drove us on to the finish line. Thanks to her and the rest of the dedicated team at Emons.

– D. D. & G. M.

Art Credits

Archibald Menzies (ch. 3): Jack Harman
Centennial Rocket Ship (ch. 15): Lew Perry
Coup DeVilla (ch. 18): Steve Edmundson
Fortes' Fountain (ch. 32): Charles Marega
Giant Metal Haida Crab (ch. 34): George Norris
Granville Island Silos (ch. 35): Osgemeos (Gustavo
    and Otavio Pandolfo)
Haida Canoe (ch. 39): Bill Reid
Harry Jerome Statue (ch. 43): Jack Harman
Huge Olympic Village Birds (ch. 52): Myfanwy Macleod
Japanese Canadian War Memorial (ch. 54): James Benzie
Rick Hansen Statue (ch. 85): William (Bill) Koochin
Visions of Possibilities (ch. 107): Robb Dunfield
Waterfront Station (ch. 108): Adelaide Langford

The authors

With pen in hand and camera strapped around his neck **Dave Doroghy** has visited over 50 different countries. Unlike most of the city's inhabitants, he was actually born in Vancouver and spent most of his life living and working downtown. His careers have spanned radio broadcasting, advertising and finally 20 years in sports marketing where he was the Vice President of the former NBA Vancouver Grizzlies and more recently the Director of Sponsorship Sales for the Vancouver 2010 Olympic Winter Games. Dave now lives on a floating home just outside of the city where he raises bees.

Graeme Menzies has lived in seven cities across Canada, in the United States, England, and Brazil, but still thinks Vancouver is the prettiest of them all. An international marketing and communications professional with past experience in the arts, public policy, technology, sport, and higher education, Graeme's curiosity fuels his passion for discovering new places and for shedding new light on old ones.

The information in this book was accurate at the time of publication, but it can change at any time. Please confirm the details for the places you're planning to visit before you head out on your adventures.